AMERICA'S FORGOTTEN COLONIAL HISTORY

DANA HUNTLEY

LYONS
PRESS

Guilford, Connecticut

An imprint of The Rowman & Littlefield Publishing Group, Inc.
4501 Forbes Blvd., Ste. 200
Lanham, MD 20706
www.rowman.com

Distributed by NATIONAL BOOK NETWORK

British Library Cataloguing in Publication Information available

Library of Congress Cataloging-in-Publication Data available

ISBN 978-1-4930-3847-3 (hardcover)
ISBN 978-1-4930-3848-0 (e-book)

♾ The paper used in this publication meets the minimum requirements of American National Standard for Information Sciences—Permanence of Paper for Printed Library Materials, ANSI/ NISO Z39.48-1992.

Printed in the United States of America

CONTENTS

Qui Esse Summas Nunc Venimus
What we are to be, we are now becoming

CONTENTS

CONTENTS

CONTENTS

And so, the thirteen British colonies born of centuries of history and the ideals of their own time made common cause in a complex world and became the United States.

Remembering the Past

To anyone in the world, a Yankee is an American. To an American, a Yankee is a Northerner. To a Northerner, a Yankee is someone from New England. To a New Englander, a Yankee is a farmer from Vermont who wears galoshes year round and eats apple pie for breakfast.

FOR A CENTURY NOW, SINCE AMERICAN INDUSTRY AND MANPOWER tipped the balance of power in World War I, America has been the dominant economic and military force among the nations of the world. Certainly the sheer size of our sea-to-shining-sea country and its physical resources helped make that possible. We have mountain ranges of metallic ore and coal. Vast arable prairies yield unimaginable quantities of grains. More than twelve thousand miles of coastline—Atlantic, Pacific and Gulf—proffer seafood of every genre. There are ranges of cattle land, broad valleys of fruit trees, and thousands of square miles of forest timber.

To this elsewhere inconceivable plentitude of natural resources, for two hundred years people have come to America from every homeland and tribe on the globe. They have built new lives for themselves. They have become American. And we don't think anything about it. Whatever our ethnic or national background, however our own DNA mix scatters ancestors about the continents, anyone who shares life here can think of themselves as American. Despite the differences of race or politics, that is a commonality we take for granted.

It has never been so in other lands. In my travels to Britain many years ago, I discovered I could move to England and settle into village life comfortably for thirty years, but I could never be "English." Friends and neighbors and the regulars down at the pub would always think of me as "the American." It would hardly be any different in Italy, China, or Morocco.

Characteristics of the commonality that makes us American include resourcefulness, initiative, a desire for upward mobility, and a society that makes that freely possible. Americans are generally hardworking, friendly, and optimistic. The blind spot Americans have in the eyes of Europeans and Asians is that we have no awareness of history, and that is because in comparative terms we have so little of it. Sadly enough, that is all too true. And becoming more so to our great detriment.

In the last three generations, our high school and college core curricula have shown a steady decrease in civics, world history, Western civilization, and United States history requirements. It has become acceptable to tear down the statues and displace the murals of our past's heroes. We cannot change the past by trying to hide it, forget it, or pretend that it didn't exist. We can only learn from it. Yes, it is important. As philosopher George Santayana so trenchantly observed, "Those who do not remember the past are condemned to repeat it."

The piece of our American history that is most lost to us is perhaps the most basic. How and why did this country get started, and how and why does its society have the characteristics that it does? The answers lie in the nation of America's prehistory. What happened between the time European adventurers first began their exploration of North America and our 1776 Declaration of Independence? As a people, we just don't know. This fundamental knowledge is simply not part of our national consciousness and mythology.

My own interest in the topic of our American roots in England began purely as an accident of birth. A few years after World War II, I was born of two New Hampshire farm families, both of which came to New England in its infancy. At that time, farm communities throughout northern New England were very Anglo. I could sing Gilbert & Sullivan choruses before I went to school, knew the stories of Robin Hood and King Arthur's knights, went to the Congregational Church, and ate baked beans on Saturday night.

Beyond a general understanding that the Pilgrims sailed here on the *Mayflower* to find religious liberty and that New Englanders were generally descended from grim Puritans, however, there was little in family or community lore, and nothing in our schooling that seriously addressed colonial history or the reasons behind the settlement of our thirteen English colonies. Let alone did I know that New England methods of building construction, my grandmothers' cooking techniques, figures of speech and idioms and the proverbs repeated to the younger generations were brought from East Anglia and the East Midlands, homeland to the majority of the region's first-generation settlers.

As way leads on to way, an academic path of study and teaching English (specifically British Literature), founding and directing a special-interest British travel company, years of writing and editing *British Heritage* magazine, and decades of purposeful travel in Britain began to put the pieces together for me.

There is always a story, and there is always a story behind the story—a backstory. The headline is that before we won our independence and became a nation in 1786, our thirteen constituent colonies were almost entirely Anglo. That is, we were English. Not only were we ethnically and culturally English, we were politically English—a part of that nation as substantially as Yorkshire and Liverpool, Bristol and London. In the early 1700s, as an English territory, we also became British, when with the Treaty of Union in 1706, Scotland, Wales, and England became Great Britain.

American colonial history from the earliest explorers until our War of Independence was inextricably woven into the broader rich tapestry of two thousand years of Britain's history. Celtic and Roman, Anglo-Saxon, Viking, and Norman: the evolution of what became the English, Scottish, and Welsh identity and political order in all its manifestations through the Middle Ages, the Enlightenment, and the Industrial Revolution is our history as well.

In the seventeenth and eighteenth centuries, what became English North America emerged as thirteen individual and to some extent self-governing colonies, each with its own story of beginnings in grant, charter, or corporation in England, and each independent of the others. Each drew settlers, saying a permanent farewell to their villages and family, crossing the Atlantic under often harsh conditions to begin life here. These early colonists, economic and religious migrants alike, were a people of faith. They came because in one fashion or another they believed fervently that they would find a better life. But a life better than what?

How did these motivations develop, and how did they find expression and fulfillment in the several varied societies that made up these, our thirteen colonies? We do not know our colonial history, because we do not know the story of English history.

We rather passively assume that having united in our Revolutionary War, we were indeed united as soon as the Founding Fathers hammered out our federal republic in Philadelphia through the 1780s. Such was not the case. Our colonies were hardly homogenous. The Puritan society that defined New England was quite different from the Cavalier establishment in the South. In between, the indelible imprint of William Penn and tolerant Quaker belief opened channels of entry for other immigrant communities in the mid-Atlantic. While these different Anglo-British identities provided a common language and belief in a better life than that they left behind in Britain, their differences in worldview, religion, social organization, and selfhood itself were marked.

It was another accident of providence that gave me an experiential understanding of just how real those differences were and the ways in which they still cast their shadows on America to this day. Had I spent my entire life and career in Red Sox Nation, the rest would have been academic—just as there is a difference between knowing all about Tokyo without ever having seen or experienced it as opposed to actually having lived there. As a young man, I spent a dozen years in the mid-Atlantic states of Pennsylvania, New Jersey, and New York. As an older man, I lived ten years in Potomac Valley, Virginia—within an hour's drive of Gettysburg, Antietam, Manassas, Harpers Ferry, and Cedar Creek. Yes, these are very different subcultures within the commonality of American experience.

Alfred, Lord Tennyson's poetic hero Ulysses voices what is true for all of us:

> "I am a part of all that I have met;
> Yet all experience is an arch wherethro'

Gleams that untravell'd world whose margin fades
Forever and forever when I move."

We are shaped by our families, the stories we hear at the knees of our parents and grandparents, our teachers, the books we read, and the life encounters we gather along the way. Inevitably, that is true of me no more or less than any other writer.

A terrible multicar accident occurs at a busy four-way intersection. It is witnessed by four people, one standing on each of the four street corners. When police take statements from the witnesses, they each describe as accurately as possible what they observed. When read separately, however, the four accounts of the accident may seem wildly disparate, even contradictory. Each of the witnesses can only report on the incident as seen from their angle of vision.

Certainly the narrative tale of America's colonial beginnings would read rather differently told by an English royalist with an ancestor who fought here against our Continental Army. No less would the story take a somewhat different cast written by a historian whose ancestors owned Virginia plantations. The best intentions of objectivity do not eliminate the matter of perspective. It seems only fair to acknowledge that reality.

Of course just as truly, every reader brings to a book their own angle of vision as well. That is why a novel, history, or biography read in our youth is not the same book when we reread it several decades later.

How well the story of our forgotten national origins shines through the perspectives of this narrative and its readers, these pages must show.

Despite our differences in philosophy and background, through the wars and debates, scandals and iniquities of American history and our colonial beginnings, the American experience is still amazing and unique—the sometimes reluctant and unexpressed envy of people throughout the world. As respected UN diplomat and prolific Indian writer Shashi Tharoor expressed it succinctly, "The unspoken slogan of many protestors outside U.S. embassies abroad is really: Yankee go home, but take me with you."

CHAPTER I

In the Beginning: A Tale of Two Countries

When in the course of human events it becomes necessary for one people to dissolve the political bands which have connected them with another and to assume among the powers of the earth, the separate and equal station to which the Laws of Nature and of Nature's God entitle them, a decent respect to the opinions of mankind requires that they should declare the causes which impel them to the separation.
— The Declaration of Independence

We all learned the same narrative of America's colonial founding. We heard it just as did our teachers, and their teachers before them.

America was first settled by the Virginia Company in Jamestown, Virginia, in 1607. John Smith was the hero of that early settlement. Then, there was that cool story about the Indian princess Pocahontas. They struggled a long time, but eventually there were lots of plantations and Virginia became the Southern colonies.

The Pilgrims on the *Mayflower* landed at Plymouth Rock in 1620. They had a rough start, but ultimately made a better go of it and celebrated with a big Thanksgiving dinner shared with the native Indians. Other uptight religious Puritans followed them and, lo, the whole place became New England.

There were some Dutch down in New York, and sooner or later William Penn and the Quakers came to build the City of Brotherly Love in Pennsylvania and . . . swoosh . . . it's 1776 and time to revolt against King George III and be America.

That's it. That's the narrative of American colonial history known to one and all.

Yet there are 150 years—six generations at least—between Plymouth Plantation and the mid-eighteenth century; that's 150 years of our national consciousness, virtually unaccounted for in our American narrative. The population colonizing English North America went from a few hundred to 2.5 million; the Atlantic seaboard became thirteen separate colonies, each with their own capital and colonial government. Philadelphia, New York, and Boston blossomed as major British trading ports. How did this happen?

These are decades of American experience that can offer wisdom to us today. With this lost history there are lost answers to the questions of who we are as an American people, and how we came to have the identity and the national consciousness that we do.

In a sense, it's rather understandable that we have forgotten this period of our national history. After all, through all those generations we were English and then British colonies. Our families and roots were in Great Britain; it was our common culture and history, commerce and language. The island three thousand miles across the North Atlantic was where our political allegiance lay and our government sprung. Even the clothing fashion of every generation was determined in London.

When our independent colonial will prevailed and the United States of America emerged, it was only natural that we promote our own American identity—the American exceptionalism that allowed us to build a nation with an entirely new concept of government, and inevitably London became less "fashionable." Family ties to the old country died out; new waves of settlers from Germany, Scandinavia, and the Mediterranean joined America's welcoming arms and created a practical multiculturalism unlike the Western world had ever seen. Though Britain and its past remained our cultural wellspring and English its much-desired tongue, the essential Englishness of our early colonial beginnings and its events simply faded into the background.

Near the town of Banbury, Sulgrave Manor was built in the mid-1500s by Laurence Washington. George's father, John Washington, emigrated from here to Virginia in 1654. Open to the public, the Manor flies the American flag in commemoration of our national connection.

We have lost the seventeenth and early eighteenth century from our history—our founding and our maturing as a people. Fewer and fewer people over the generations have been able to make sense of that history. Who, what, when, where, and why were people motivated to make a three-month crossing on the North Atlantic aboard ships most of us wouldn't take out on the Chesapeake, knowing they would never see home or family again, to land on and carve a life in a largely uncharted, sparsely inhabited wilderness? How and why did they build the varied societies that they did here in the New World colonies? How and why did they become America? How did they become us?

The answers lie back in England. It took me decades of traveling the length and breadth of the island of Great Britain to appreciate just how deeply. Almost every town and city in Britain marks its connections to America, from Sulgrave Manor in Northamptonshire that was home to George Washington's ancestors, to the Market Place in Wells where William Penn preached, to the dozens of towns and villages across East Anglia that lent their place-names to new communities in Massachusetts Bay Colony—such as Ipswich and Barnstable, Groton and Sudbury, Hingham and Essex.

This narrative isn't a proper history, simply a retelling of the tale. The story unfolds as a rich tapestry of intrepid people motivated to move across the ocean under sail to an unknown, expansive wilderness and an often hostile environment because of climate and a volatile and often violent indigenous people they were displacing.

They were motivated to migrate for economic, political, family, and personal reasons, but the overarching motivation of seventeenth-century migration that stamped its character on the development of our several and united colonies was religion.

It makes a fascinating story, because there is an element of unreality to it. In our generally "enlightened" and tolerant twenty-first century, we find it difficult to perceive that Christian differences in church belief, practice, and worship liturgy should cause two hundred years of warfare, persecution, torture, and judicial murder. Less pejoratively expressed, we find it difficult to understand how these things should be considered as important as they were. But they were, and the religious convictions of Anglicans, Congregationalists, Quakers, Catholics, Presbyterians, and Anabaptists all reverberate in our national and regional cultures to this day.

For proper history, I have been enlightened by the narratives of Winston Churchill, Paul Johnson, Peter Ackroyd, and a cast of many. The one who knows, however, and lucidly writes the history is Brandeis historian David Hackett Fischer, whose *Albion's Seed* and *Liberty and Freedom* have long inspired my own reflections.

"History" is the cause and effect of the human race; one thing leads to another. It has always been thus. The conundrum anyone writing about history (that would be historiography*) faces is determining where to start their account. American colonial history, though, inevitably begins in England. So, the question is where there to begin.*

—————

4

Over the last few decades, the populist American vision has been to ignore, denigrate, and overlook the very nature of America's root ethos. Like Canada, New Zealand, and Australia, we were a settlement colony. We are wrapped in the silken bond Winston Churchill called simply "the English-speaking Peoples."

Of course, there is a uniqueness to our American identity. After all, we were the first nation in the world formed as an explicitly Protestant country. The documents of America's founding, the Declaration of Independence and the Constitution, are the first instruments of government that were born out of a Reformation worldview. For all the other countries of "Western Civilization," regardless of their religious or irreligious culture since the Enlightenment, their history lies in the medieval Catholicism that was indeed roughly "universal," throughout Europe at least, until the sixteenth century.

> *To Americans, a hundred years is a long time; to the British, a hundred miles is a long distance.*

What we lack here in America is *any* sense of history. For decades I have been describing the difference between British and Americans thus: To Americans, a hundred years is a long time; to the British, a hundred miles is a long distance.

Here's a brief imaginary journey. Along the coast of northern Massachusetts spilling over into New Hampshire, buildings stand in Ipswich, Newburyport, and Portsmouth that have been residences, taverns, and churches since the 1600s. Down in Virginia, every market town invites visitors to their "historic district," which simply means that they have standing buildings predating our own Civil War—mid-nineteenth century. Travel out to Tulsa, Tucson, or Tacoma and try to find a structure built before 1900.

That's it. On our soil we can carve out a few hundred years, and often we don't even think of history in terms beyond that. Because our nation began proximately in 1776, our national emotional intelligence begins our history then. Speaking in the broadest of generalizations, that is why to the nations of the world we often appear naïve and slapdash in our attitudes. They simply grow up with a longer, deeper frame of reference, and we are still regarded as the new kids on the block—with a chip on our shoulder. It is not like that, of course. We do have a history; we've simply chosen rather passively to ignore it.

In one sense, we can date our history, now eight hundred years, to the sealing of Magna Carta on the meadows of Runnymede in June 1215. There beside the River Thames a few miles from Windsor, King John was forced to acquiesce to his barons and recognize rights under law that superseded the king's prerogative. In broad terms, it established rule by law; it determined that the monarch (read chief executive officer) govern *under* the law, and not as its personal wellspring.

Magna Carta was the beginning of jurisprudence and the rule of law as we understand it in the English-speaking nations (and much of the Western world), and is thus the meaningful charter of American history. The meadow at Runnymede is still a meadow today, on the busy A308 between Windsor and Staines. In a copse behind the field stands the Magna Carta memorial—a rotunda and plinth—inscribed with the legend "In Memory of Magna Carta—Foundation of Law." Pointedly, the memorial was raised in 1957, and is maintained to this day, by the American Bar Association.

It was a long, bloody, and hard struggle to get from Magna Carta in the thirteenth century to a contemporary understanding of representative democracy, and to our rule of law under the Constitution of the United States. In a matter of months, both King John and the barons reneged on their assurances in that treaty.

Several decades later, the Second Baron's War, fought over its principles, prompted England's effectual ruler of the time, Simon de Montfort, eighth Earl of Leicester, to call for the first elected Parliament of what became the Commons. Known as the "Father of Parliament," de Montfort died in the Battle of Evesham (1265), but Magna Carta and ultimately Parliament lived on. Every successive king for two hundred

The Magnitude of Magna Carta

What has become known as Magna Carta—the Great Charter—
has been recognized almost since its inception (not only by the
British but all the English-speaking settler nations) as a seminal
document on the slow road to constitutional, representative
government.

The charter King John was forced to seal under duress at
Runnymede in 1215 did not create any judicial rights for the
great majority of his subjects. The powerful landed nobility had
little thought for the common tenants who worked their land
and occupied their villages. The rights that the barons—the
kingdom's feudal tenants-in-chief—insisted upon codifying and
protecting were their own. What Magna Carta did do, however,
was acknowledge that the monarch was subject to the law and
not above it—or worse still, that the king could make or change
law by personal fiat.

In what was essentially a treaty, its provisions prohibited
imprisonment without charge and provided for swift adjudica-
tion—the basis of habeas corpus. It bound the king not to take
any extrajudicial action against persons or property, or to tax
the barons without their consent. It also provided a measure of
legal protection to cities, boroughs, and ports, denying the king's
authority to arbitrarily curtail their liberties.

Over eight hundred years, time has claimed most of the
original thirteenth-century handwritten transcriptions of Magna
Carta. Today only four copies remain extant. Two of them belong
to the British Library; one copy is virtually illegible from dam-
age by fire in 1731. The better copy is on public display in the
Treasures Gallery at the British Library near London's St. Pan-
cras Station. A third copy belongs to thirteenth-century Salisbury
Cathedral. It is on permanent display in Salisbury Cathedral's
Chapter House. The fourth surviving 1215 Magna Carta belongs
to Lincoln Cathedral. Their copy has toured the world, lent out a
number of times to highlight exhibitions on its historic threads.
Now, it is displayed in a new state-of-the-art exhibition vault
within the walls of Lincoln Castle.

There can be no more telling a symbol of America's descent from the centuries of conflict and changing intellectual history in England that gave us common roots in the foundations of law and representative government than the Magna Carta Memorial beside the meadow of Runnymede where Magna Carta was sealed.

years was forced to reissue Magna Carta in one form or another—until Parliament was established enough to codify its provisions and the document itself evolved into what became known as English Common Law.

Through the five centuries between when poor old King John was compelled to seal Magna Carta and the first permanent settlers landed on these western Atlantic shores lots of things happened. Bit by bit, English history records the movement of a people and an ethos that evolved from rule by monarchal decree and worth-by-birth to a world we recognize today. You can look it up!

For the Atlantic colonies that became America, though, our story really begins on a battlefield in the East Midlands of England in 1485.

A Helpful Transatlantic Lexicon

It is easier to follow the story with an understanding of the specific uses of Old Country place-names.

Great Britain, or Britain, is the island—largest of the British Isles. It is comprised of the southern kingdom of England, the northern kingdom of Scotland and the western historic principality of Wales. Each has its own identity, history, and national culture. From the time of the Norman Conquest, England had the dominant population, wealth, power, and feudal overlordship of Scotland and Wales. Centuries of warfare and ripples of dynastic conflict marked the island's history for eight hundred years before the twentieth-century emergence of the United Kingdom, defined by the addition of the province of Northern Ireland to Great Britain.

The unit of local government in Britain that corresponds to our states is the county. Place-names in Britain are most often identified by locality and historical county, such as Canterbury, Kent; Peterborough, Cambridgeshire; or Winchester, Hampshire.

Population or form of local government has nothing to do with the distinction between a town and a city. Though today, city status is a designated honor, historically, a city was a place that had a cathedral. The headquarters of a church diocese and the seat of its bishop made a city. In the medieval world, this alone made them centers of wealth and political power. The smallest cathedral city in Britain is St. David's, Pembrokeshire, Wales—population eighteen hundred.

CHAPTER 2

The Backstory: Britain's Rocky Reformation Sets the Stage

There is a tide in the affairs of men, which taken at the flood, leads on to fortune. Omitted, all the voyage of their life is bound in shallows and in miseries. On such a full sea are we now afloat. And we must take the current when it serves, or lose our ventures.

—WILLIAM SHAKESPEARE

ON A BATTLEFIELD IN THE ENGLISH MIDLANDS
The motivations and causes behind the English settlement of the Atlantic seaboard in the 1600s, and the differing ways that society evolved in the several American colonies, began long before the first colonists reached these shores. Historical currents always incubate long before they emerge into dramatic events.

Our story really begins on the battlefield near Market Bosworth, Leicestershire, in August 1485. History knows it as the Battle of Bosworth Field. The battle effectively ended the generation-long Wars of the Roses, an interfamily conflict between the houses of Lancaster and York, branches of Plantagenets descended from King Edward III. The Yorkist King Richard III was killed in the battle against Henry Tudor, the Earl of Richmond and last feasible Lancastrian to challenge for the throne. Tudor took Richard's crown and proclaimed himself King Henry VII.

Historians have long considered Bosworth Field the last great medieval battle. Though there is evidence of early firearms, this was the last time battle was drawn between opposing armies of fully caparisoned, armored heavy cavalry. The war had preoccupied and decimated England's nobility for more than a generation. It also ended three hundred years of Plantagenet dynasty and ushered in both the Tudors and the Renaissance.

That's the nickel version. But it wasn't quite that simple for the new King Henry VII. All the battles and bloodshed that ended with his victory over Richard III came in an era when almost everyone took for granted the divine right of kings. In that worldview, the king was God's anointed, God's appointed to rule a people—in many eyes, God's effective viceroy in the temporal kingdom. Regicide, the killing of the king, was quite simply the most horrendous sin and heinous crime that could be committed.

Henry VII was king by right of conquest, not by right of birth. Regicide took one out of the spiritual protection of the church; Henry Tudor was fair game. A goodly percentage of the arms-bearing subjects of the new king would not have felt any moral necessity to support Henry, nor to oppose those who would overthrow him. There were plenty of the latter around. While there were many royal accomplishments in Henry VII's reign, the great preoccupation of his years on the throne was protecting it, consolidating his power—and passing the throne on intact to his legitimate heir.

KING HENRY VII'S DYNASTIC PASSION PLAY

As for Richard III, his battered body was surreptitiously taken to Leicester and dumped with the brothers of Greyfriars Abbey. They buried the royal corpse in the abbey church in an unmarked grave. The story has all come to light in recent years with the highly unlikely discovery of his skeletal remains in late summer 2012, and with their ceremonial reburial in a royal tomb at Leicester Cathedral in 2015. At the time, however, the last thing Henry Tudor needed was for the tomb of the ex-king to become a place of pilgrimage and rallying symbol for his enemies.

Passing the throne on to an heir was, in fact, the only way Henry Tudor could legitimize his own reign and that of his dynasty on the English throne. The stigma of his conquest would be erased. As these things happen, Henry had two sons, both of whom he raised from infancy to bear the responsibilities of power and learn the lessons of princes. Perhaps

Lost for more than five hundred years, the remains of King Richard III were amazingly located by a team of archaeologists from the University of Leicester beneath a civic parking lot in the bustling modern city. While the circumstantial evidence might have been enough to conclude the identity of the skeletal remains, it was DNA testing that provided ultimate proof.

the greatest and most influential of these lessons was that the prime obligation of kingship was to assure the legitimate succession.

The prime obligation of kingship was to assure the legitimate succession.

Henry VII named his oldest son Arthur, born a year after Henry seized the crown in 1486. Arthurian romance was all the literary rage in the late fifteenth century. Henry deliberately hoped to tap into the currents of nationalism and pride reflected in the sage, heroic King Arthur of ancient legend. His second son, named Henry after him, was born in 1491 and intended for the church. In Henry VII's grand vision, as Arthur became king, his younger brother would be elevated to Archbishop of Canterbury, giving the family effective control of both church and state.

Henry VII's campaign to fulfill this vision of his reign and legitimize his dynasty was well-orchestrated, at least in his own mind. Henry was an early master at spin and PR. Yes, a part of that campaign was to encourage a popular view of Richard III as a tyrant that had needed to be dethroned and of himself as an instrument of good for government and for the people. A century later, Shakespeare's history-cum-tragedy *Richard III* (circa 1592) still served that Tudor cause.

The coup de grace for Henry, though, was negotiating the marriage of young Prince Arthur to the Spanish princess, Catherine, youngest daughter of Queen Isabella of Castile and King Ferdinand of Aragon, and kin to the Holy Roman Emperor. It was to Henry's and England's advantage to make such a marriage pact, forming an Anglo-Spanish alliance to counter France.

So, Prince Arthur and Catherine were married and shuttled off to Ludlow Castle in the Welsh Marches for a honeymoon in 1502—whereupon Prince Arthur soon died. This was, of course, a disaster for Henry VII's plans. Fortunately, he did have Prince Henry waiting in the wings as a spare. Now that Henry was the heir to the throne, there was little reason for England and Spain to waste the newly negotiated alliance. So, Henry was soon betrothed to Catherine of Aragon in his brother's stead (though he was only eleven at the time) and assumed the primary responsibility for producing a legitimate heir.

I'M HENRY VIII, I AM

In due course, Henry VII died, and in 1509 the second son, intended for the Church, succeeded to the throne as King Henry VIII instead, at age eighteeen. He promptly married Catherine of Aragon and was crowned in Westminster Abbey the next day.

The years rolled by and Catherine, unremarkably for the time, had a succession of miscarriages, still births, and infant deaths. She delivered only one daughter that survived, the Princess Mary. Henry began to get uneasy as Catherine's childbearing years grew short. And then he began to get desperate. Henry himself aged from being an athletic young buck and playboy to being a corpulent, demanding monarch. He became increasingly preoccupied with the reality that he had received no male heir by Queen Catherine.

Through the late 1520s Henry proposed that his marriage to his brother's widow was illegitimate on grounds of consanguinity. The Pope didn't agree and would not annul his marriage to Catherine of Aragon. Henry appealed to the theological faculties of Europe. There were several years of dickering and frustrating negotiation, and then Henry's change came. The old Archbishop of Canterbury, primate of England, died, and Henry succeeded in sliding into his office the pliable Thomas Cranmer.

With Cranmer's cooperation, Henry declared himself, not the Pope, to be the supreme head of the Church in England. In 1533, with the Act of Supremacy, Parliament agreed. The king's marriage to Catherine was annulled; the Queen was deposed, with the title Princess Dowager, and she and her daughter, Mary, were shuttled off to a quiet retirement far from the court.

Anne Boleyn, the sister of the king's mistress (and one of Queen Catherine's ladies-in-waiting) Mary Boleyn, was waiting to take her place—and promptly did. Over the next few years, Anne delivered Henry another daughter, Elizabeth, and had a couple of miscarriages, but there was no son. By now, Henry was beginning to get paranoid, and he was tired of the spirited and independent-minded Anne.

In May 1536 Anne and five young men, including her brother, lost their heads on what are regarded as most certainly trumped-up charges of adultery. That freed Henry to marry another enticing lady of the court, Jane Seymour. In short order, Jane did finally deliver to a jubilant Henry the son for whom he was desperate: Edward. Unhappily, Jane died in childbirth. Perhaps unsurprisingly, it is said that the king loved her best of all his wives.

In the meantime, all of Henry's machinations with Catherine of Aragon and the Pope (who had excommunicated him) and the Catholic Church gave Henry some significant political problems in the turbulent religious climate of the sixteenth century. England's King Henry VIII was never actually a Protestant himself, but he certainly needed Protestant allies now.

Henry's busy diplomatic service negotiated a marriage with the minor German Princess, Anne of Cleeves, to align England with the

At the Tower of London on the banks of the Thames, both Queen Anne Boleyn and Queen Catherine Howard were beheaded on Tower Green. The central keep adjacent to it is the White Tower, standing since the reign of William the Conqueror and the oldest edifice in London.

Lutheran German states. When Anne of Cleeves arrived in England for the wedding, Henry chivalrously went to meet his new bride—and took an instant dislike to her. Anne's appearance had been depicted to Henry in a rather more favorable light than she appeared to him in person. Besides, he complained, she smelled and did not bathe. It is regarded highly doubtful that the subsequent marriage was ever consummated, and Anne was quickly shuffled out of sight to Richmond Palace to live out a comfortable, invisible nonexistence. The marriage was quietly annulled.

Besides, the foxy young Catherine Howard, daughter of one of his nobles, was waiting in the wings. Henry married her, but by now the aging king, now approaching fifty, was hardly a salubrious bedmate for a lively maiden of sixteen or seventeen. She found no attraction in the corpulent, sedentary, and demanding king. Catherine's eye soon roved, followed by the rest of her. Henry was quite disappointed at having to send the pretty young queen and her lover, Thomas Culpeper, to the headsman.

King Henry VIII's metamorphosis from dashing young sportsman to grouchy, grossly overweight invalid had been spurred by a riding accident in 1536 that left Henry with a leg injury from which he never healed. The

King Henry's Schizophrenic Theology

Having been raised by his father for the Church, Henry VIII had received a thorough theological education (particularly for a layman). Henry had no sympathy for the new Lutheran heresies emanating from the Continent. In 1521 he wrote a book, *Assertio Septum Sacramentorum Adversus Martinum Lutherum*, which averred a strong loyalty to the papacy. As a result, Pope Leo X gave him the title of Defender of the Faith.

When Henry denied papal primacy in England in 1532 and became himself head of the national Church, his theology (and strident antipathy to Lutheranism) did not otherwise change. While in later years, Henry's theological musings modified his beliefs on clerical celibacy, transubstantiation, and the authority of the Church in secular affairs, he continued to regard himself a thoroughly devout Catholic throughout his life.

leg became ulcerated and kept the monarch literally off his feet for months that more or less stretched to years. Needless to say, his enforced sedentary lifestyle was not accompanied by a change in diet and eating habits. He married nice Protestant Catherine Parr, who nursed him through to his death in 1552, and then she married the man she really loved.

The simplest rubric of Henry VIII's six wives has long been remembered: divorced, beheaded, died; divorced, beheaded, survived.

EXODUS AND EXECUTION UNDER QUEEN MARY

King Henry's son, as he and his own father dreamed, carried on the legitimate succession that motivated both their lives. Edward VI became king at the tender age of ten. He was to be guided to his majority by Protestant regents, most notably the able Duke of Somerset. Unhappily a sickly lad, Edward never reached his majority, dying at sixteen of tuberculosis ("consumption") in 1558. As both Henry Tudors learned and Robert Burns penned, "the best laid plans of mice and men gang oft aglee."

It must be one of the great ironies of history. After all the devices of Henry VIII to fulfill the prime directive received from his own father, his daughter, not a son, took the throne of England. Whether Europe was ready for a female monarch or not, they got one. Mary Tudor, daughter of the humiliated and cast-aside Catherine of Aragon, became Queen Mary. Oops.

> *They could return to the Catholic Church; they could go into exile; they could die a painful death at the stake as heretics and apostates.*

Mary had been in exile with her mother for more than a decade, sharing her mother's shame and bearing her own with the label of bastardy. As was her Spanish mother, Mary was devoutly Roman Catholic throughout this English "Reformation" to advance her father's ends. She assumed the crown in 1553 full of righteous indignation and bitter resentment, determined that her holy duty as queen was to return England to the bosom of the Catholic Church.

The faction in the Church of England that had remained true to the Catholic faith in the midst of Henry's upheavals cheered Mary's devout stand for the "true religion." For almost everyone else, Mary's five-year reign was a nightmare. This return to Catholicism was not optional for her subjects. In essence, they were faced with three choices. They could return to the Catholic Church; they could go into exile; they could die a painful death at the stake as heretics and apostates.

Out in the counties, the villages, and the small towns of England, practical religion had often not changed much over the intervening decades. The parish church was served by the village priest. The church may have been the only stone building in town, and in many places, the priest the only literate man. The tumult of King Henry VIII's political and religious problems did not touch their everyday life. That church governance business was played out by the upper echelons of the episcopacy—far removed from rural parishes where most English folk lived.

These ordinary people were naturally Catholic, as had been their ancestors from time immemorial. Then, Henry became the national pontiff, and they were told that they were, well, kinda, sorta Protestant. Now, under Queen Mary, they were directed that they were Catholic again. They became Catholic easily enough, because what they were taught, what they believed, and how they worshipped had never changed to begin with.

But it wasn't so easy for everyone. The winds of Reformation had long been blowing in England. Oxford cleric John Wycliffe had stirred that wind back in the 1300s, and been persecuted for his translation of the Bible into the English language of the people, and his questioning of the authority of the Pope and the Roman curacy. His followers, called Lollards, had spread Wycliffe's startling doctrines through the country before the ecclesiastical establishment successfully suppressed them.

After Henry's break from Rome, Protestant thought took hold particularly (and understandably, given the geography) in East Anglia and the counties of the East Midlands. Cambridge University was a hotbed of Protestant ideas making their way from the Continent (and the nearby

The Wycliffe Bible

An Oxford don, cleric, and theologian, John Wycliffe (1329–1384), was dissatisfied with the Church of his day and became convinced the Bible should be available to people in the vernacular of their own English tongue. Over several years to publication in its entirety in 1382, Wycliffe and a small number of unknown translators conspiring with him rendered the complete Latin Vulgate word-for-word into English—the first translation of the Bible into the English language. It was a functional translation, but often very obscure and unreadable. The original "edition" was published and subsequently copied by hand for some sixty years before print. The Wycliffe Bible was suppressed by the Catholic Church. Wycliffe died two years later, before the persecution could catch up with him.

Netherlands in particular). Along the eastern coast of England, there were many priests and young scholarly laymen who chose exile under Queen Mary's ultimatum rather than face the alternatives. Where they went, again understandably enough, was Zurich, Geneva, and Frankfurt—the centers of Protestant thought and Reformed theology.

Left in England was a remnant for whom neither forced conversion to Catholicism nor exile from Britain was a practical or moral option. For those, Mary was as good as her word. Many scores of individuals were put to death for failing to recant their Protestant faith, often by burning at the stake, commonly with inhuman physical torture a prelude to death. Perhaps the most famous of these were the trio of Anglican bishops—Nicholas Ridley, Hugh Latimer, and Archbishop of Canterbury Thomas Cranmer—whose death at the stake is commemorated by Martyrs Memorial, one of the most iconic landmarks in Oxford. These were the years recorded in the famous Foxe's *Book of Martyrs*. This is the Queen known as Bloody Mary.

The bitter queen found herself in the same situation that her father had been in—in the crosshairs of Europe's tense religious politics. She was the untested "frail female" monarch, who needed to make a politically advantageous marriage—and did, to King Philip II of Spain, Europe's most powerful Catholic monarch. On her part, Mary loved Philip dearly. He saw her island as a prize, and sent a surrogate to stand in for him at the wedding.

Philip never actually lived with Mary in England at all, although he visited from time to time. A few years went by and the court and the country began to expect Mary to get pregnant and deliver an heir to the throne. So did she. At last, Queen Mary began to show signs of a baby bump, and she let it get around that she was indeed with child.

In Biblical phrase, the time was accomplished when she should be delivered, yet no baby made an appearance. As the days stretched into weeks, Mary began to be a laughing stock of the court and beyond. Her supposed pregnancy had masked a more somber reality: Queen Mary's bump was a tumor. She died of the cancerous growth, in humiliation, only months later, in 1558.

THE CHILD OF REFORMATION BRINGS PROTESTANT ASCENDENCY

In the meantime, Mary's half sister, Elizabeth, had been living quietly away from the court and limelight. It was only by the most skillful exercise of her wits that she remained untouched by the religious passions of the day—and kept her own head. Now, that head in its turn would wear England's crown.

Elizabeth, daughter of Anne Bolyen, already called the Child of the Reformation, came to the throne in her own right as England's first Protestant monarch. With the exception of the relatively small number of devout, committed Catholics, most of England breathed a collective sigh of relief. While Elizabeth was loyal to the Church of England, her church was a Protestant one, outside the sphere of the Pope and the Church of Rome. Little else was yet decided.

Now in the last decades of the sixteenth century, the English Reformation really began.

With the young Protestant queen and a secure Protestant ascendancy, however, those hundreds of conscience exiles to the Continent were free to come home to England. While they left under the clouds of persecution, though, they returned with missionary zeal. Those years in places such as the Zurich of Ulrich Zwengli and the Geneva of John Calvin had schooled them in Reformation theology and sharpened their conviction in the worldview-changing Protestant doctrines: *sola fide, sola gratia, sola scriptura*: only faith, only grace, only Scripture.

These men had fled to the Continent as individual refugees of conscience. They returned to East Anglia, to London and the Midlands—and to Cambridge—with an identity and a sense of purpose. The Church of England had been taken out of the Church of Rome. Now, it was time to take Rome out of the Anglican Church. These were the Puritans. Now, in the last decades of the sixteenth century, the English Reformation really began.

CHAPTER 3

Queen Elizabeth and a New World

I do not so much rejoice that God hath made me to be a Queen, as to be a Queen over so thankful a people.

—ELIZABETH I

QUEEN ELIZABETH (SHE DIDN'T BECOME "I," OF COURSE, UNTIL THERE was a Queen Elizabeth II) took the throne facing a difficult realm and a dangerous world for England. Religious upheaval and religiously inspired conflict shuddered through Europe as clear lines had been drawn on the religious map. The Germanic states and Alsace, Switzerland, Scandinavia, and the Netherlands became Protestant. The Mediterranean countries remained Roman Catholic. The most powerful of those was Spain—with dire grievances against England for its treatment of Catherine of Aragon and her daughter, and for its national apostasy against the true Church. Besides, Philip II never did manage to get his hands on England.

Elizabeth had her own foibles and blind spots, certainly. In sum, however, she navigated the shoals of sixteenth-century geopolitics with aplomb. As well she knew, she herself was the biggest prize in the international commodity market. Elizabeth's marriage into one of the royal European houses would ipso facto create a formidable alliance. And so, Elizabeth kept Europe, as well as her own interested nobility, waiting. For two decades she kept them waiting, flirting first with one, then another, possibility. Throughout, she shared a lifelong flirtation (at least) with childhood playmate Robert Dudley, whom she named the Earl of Leicester.

When it came to religion, Elizabeth was equally savvy and noncommittal. She clearly supported the basic tenets of Protestantism, and she unambiguously supported the episcopacy of the Church of England hierarchy. That left two groups on the outside. There remained, if not quite underground, then a markedly subdued and wisely low-profile cadre of committed Catholic movers and shakers. The Catholic Church itself went underground. Its missionary Jesuit priests were outlawed, seized on discovery, exiled, and sometimes executed.

There were also those whose Reformation conviction saw no good in the ecclesiastical hierarchy of the Anglican Church, whose doctrine of the Church itself, ecclesiology in theological parlance, was Presbyterian or Congregational. They returned from the Continent to England as Dissenters, or soon enough would become such.

MEANWHILE, NORTH IN SCOTLAND

The Reformation happened differently, and earlier, in Scotland. King James V was married into the French royal family. His wife, Mary of Guise, was devoutly Catholic. Undercurrents of Protestant thought stirred up nobles and populace alike from the early 1540s. The leading and outspoken spokesman for these heretical ideas was renegade priest George Wisheart, who preached against such Catholic doctrines as Purgatory, prayers for the dead, and more. One of his young followers was an increasingly likeminded priest who served as bodyguard for Wisheart— John Knox.

In 1546 the ecclesiastical authorities caught up with George Wisheart, tried him for heresy, and burned him at the stake. A few months later, Protestant revolutionaries murdered the Catholic prelate of Scotland, Cardinal Beaton, in revenge for Wisheart's death. A brief rebellion ensued. The Protestant rebels holed up in St. Andrews Castle on the North Sea coast. Knox had escaped Wisheart's apprehension and fate, and joined the Protestants at St. Andrews.

The advantage of the French alliance for the Stuarts was the availability of French troops, with whose assistance the resistance at St. Andrews was crushed. John Knox was taken prisoner by the French and spent the next nineteen months as a French galley slave. When he was released in

1649, Knox found it expedient to hightail it to England, where he was licensed in the Church of England. He took a parish in Buckinghamshire, but Knox's reputation had preceded him to a royal circle trying to solidify a Protestant court, and the next year Knox was appointed chaplain to the teenage King Edward VI.

When young Edward died at sixteen, the new Catholic Queen Mary's court was no place for John Knox. Like so many others, Knox fled to the Continent. He went to Geneva, where he sat under the teaching of John Calvin and made his friendship. Later he moved to Frankfurt with Calvin's blessing to pastor the congregation of English exiles there. A rift arose over the liturgy. While new arrivals from England brought the familiar High Church liturgy to which they were accustomed, those who had been there awhile, including Knox, had adopted the new Reformed liturgy of Geneva.

John Knox returned to Scotland and became the spiritual leader and strident voice of the growing group of Protestant Scottish nobility, who came to be called the Lords of the Congregation. King James V had died in 1542, leaving the Scottish throne to his only child, Mary, still a toddler. The regency lay in the hands of her mother, Mary of Guise, the French princess.

At age three, Mary, even then Queen of Scots, was sent to be brought up with her mother's family in the French court. Mary did not see the country of which she was queen again until she was twenty-one. Mary of Guise took on a multiyear struggle to maintain Scotland as a loyal Catholic country. She was increasingly isolated, unpopular, and ultimately unsuccessful.

By the time Mary of Guise died and her daughter, Mary Queen of Scots, returned from the Continent to reign in her own right, Scotland was lost—an overwhelmingly and enthusiastic Protestant country. While a teenager in Paris, Mary had been wedded to the Dauphin Francois, heir to the French throne and briefly the king. He was a sickly lad, however, and soon died; Mary arrived home a widow and one of Europe's most eligible ladies. She was also thoroughly Catholic in her upbringing and her loyalties.

FOLLIES OF THE QUEEN OF SCOTS

Just up the thoroughfare, now known as the Royal Mile, from Queen Mary Stuart's lodgings at the Palace of Holyroodhouse, John Knox occupied the bully pulpit of Scotland: St. Giles Cathedral. While traditionally known as St. Giles Cathedral, in actuality, the church was only a cathedral for a short period of its history. No bishop has sat enthroned in St. Giles from Knox's day to this. St. Giles is formally styled the High Kirk of Edinburgh. From its pulpit, Knox kept up the pressure on the hapless Queen Mary.

A foolish marriage to a noble wastrel (and her cousin), Lord Darnley, did nothing to aid her reputation. His murder a few years later was not much mourned. Mary's reputed implication in the atrocity left her further isolated. She found a champion in the Earl of Bothwell, who became her third husband. Bothwell was a randy and renegade border laird who did not lack panache. He did, however, lack the political and military muscle that it would have taken to solidify Mary's position as a ruling and respected monarch. Eventually, Mary fled to England, hoping to seek succor from her kinswoman and fellow female monarch Queen Elizabeth. Bothwell scampered off to the Continent, where he died in Denmark broken and destitute.

In 1560 the Scottish Parliament asked John Knox and five other ministers to draw up a Reformed statement of faith and statement of polity for the Scottish Kirk. The result, returned to Parliament in only five days, was the Scots Confession, generally accepted as having been written largely by Knox. It was adopted by Parliament; the Scottish Presbyterian Kirk was born. In Scotland, at least, the Reformation was accomplished. The Scots Confession remains a part of the Presbyterian Book of Confessions today.

Elizabeth was hardly going to commit resources, let alone troops, to restoring a Catholic monarch to a virulently Presbyterian neighbor—kin or not.

Depictions of early Protestant reformers such as Ulrich Zwengli, John Calvin, and John Knox, here in St. Giles Cathedral, show them with long, untrimmed beards. This was not simply a matter of style, but an intentional and visible mark of their "protest." Priests and monastic brothers of the Roman Catholic Church were required to be clean-shaven.

Mary, Queen of Scots, meanwhile, did not get the reception in England that she was expecting. From the moment she arrived, Mary was seen as nothing but a threat to Queen Elizabeth. With the Spanish and other Catholic sharks swarming on the Continent, and her own nobility increasingly solidified in a Protestant Church of England, Elizabeth was hardly going to commit resources, let alone troops, to restoring a Catholic monarch to a virulently Presbyterian neighbor—kin or not.

On Mary's side, her protestations of loyalty to Elizabeth were in vain. As Elizabeth's advisors, most particularly Sir William Cecil, reminded her constantly: As long as Mary was in the country, she was a focal point for stirring up Catholic hostility, including attempts to place Mary, Elizabeth's heir presumptive, on the English throne. Mary was just dangerous. As a result, her northern English retreat morphed from courteous hospitality into house arrest, and Mary was kept under guard for eighteen years.

Mary herself, understandably enough, was only too willing to cooperate with attempts to free her and return her to Scotland and her throne. Elizabeth resisted her advisors' counsel to eliminate Mary and the threat. At last, however, Elizabeth was confronted with incontrovertible evidence that Mary was in collusion on a plot that if successful would have ended Elizabeth's life. With great reluctance and sadness, Elizabeth was eventually convinced to sign the warrant for the execution of Mary, Queen of Scots. She was beheaded at Fotheringhay Castle, Northamptonshire, in June of 1585.

The result of Mary's demise was the accession to the Scottish throne of her one young son by Lord Darnley. When Mary fled to England, the toddler Stuart prince, James, had been taken in charge by the controlling Protestant nobility that formed the regency council, led by the Earl of Mar. The Stuart heir was raised to kingship and in the Presbyterian faith. He had little contact with the common folk and had been given a keen sense of his own importance. He was now King James VI of Scotland. And Scotland was an overwhelmingly Presbyterian country.

EXPANDING THE ELIZABETHAN WORLD

Much more, of course, was going on during the busy reign of Queen Elizabeth. The last decades of the 1500s were the great age of Atlantic exploration—and the claiming of territory to the west in the New World.

The last decades of the 1500s were the great age of Atlantic exploration—and the claiming of territory to the west in the New World.

Though Christopher Columbus made his famous transatlantic voyage in 1492, what he discovered was the Caribbean islands and subsequently Central America. Six years later, John Cabot sailed the Atlantic west aboard the *Matthew* from Bristol. Cabot found North America in 1498 and laid claim to large swathes of the new landmass's Atlantic seaboard for England.

In Elizabeth's reign, it was the Caribbean, however, that made a prime battleground between England, Spain, and occasionally France. While the Spanish searched for El Dorado and plunder to carry back to Spain, the English were interested in the islands for sugar plantations. These were the days of the privateers. Elizabeth commissioned swashbucklers such as Sir Francis Drake to harass and rob the Spanish and act as surrogates for her interests.

THE VANISHING COLONY OF ROANOKE ISLAND

The first attempt to build an English settlement community in North America was commissioned by Queen Elizabeth in 1584. Sir Walter Raleigh was chartered with the mission of funding and planning the project. Raleigh's intentions were to harvest profitable goods such as sassafras from the area and to make his colony a base for privateering against the Spanish. After a couple of scouting expeditions and faltering starts, in 1587 a group of 115 intrepid colonists—men, women, and children—under the governorship of Captain John White, a friend of Raleigh's, established themselves at Roanoke Island on the Outer Banks of present-day North Carolina.

That summer White's daughter Elizabeth gave birth on Roanoke Island to a daughter, Virginia Dare, who was thus the first English child born in the New World. A few months later, a dearth of supplies and hostilities with local Indians convinced Captain White to return to

Sir Walter Raleigh:
Elizabethan Swashbuckler

Born of a well-connected Devonshire manorial family in the early 1550s, Walter Raleigh's upbringing was decidedly and passionately Protestant. His father barely escaped execution under Queen Mary. While details of his young life are sketchy, as a young man Raleigh served as a mercenary supporting the Huguenots in France from 1569 to 1575. For his work in the suppression of Irish rebellions from 1579 to 1583, he was richly rewarded with Irish land, and in 1584 Queen Elizabeth granted Raleigh a broad charter to explore, colonize, and exploit any unclaimed territory in the New World. Elizabeth's quid pro quo was that she got one-fifth of the silver and gold extracted there. The failed and vanished colony of Roanoke Island was part of the result, but Raleigh had other irons in the fire.

Knighted by the queen in 1585, Sir Walter sat in Parliament for Devonshire, was made Lord Lieutenant of Cornwall, and given a vice-admiralship. Over the next fifteen years, Raleigh led an expedition to South America in search of the elusive El Dorado, fought the Spanish at sea on a number of occasions, served as governor of the Island of Jersey, and moved in and out of favor with Queen Elizabeth.

After the queen's death in 1603, Raleigh's fortunes turned worse under King James I. Raleigh was arrested that summer for his alleged involvement in a conspiracy against the king, tried and convicted of treason on what is taken to be hearsay evidence. After being held in the Tower of London for thirteen years, Raleigh was paroled by the king in 1617 to lead another voyage to Venezuela in search of El Dorado—on condition that he not engage in any hostile action against Spanish ships or colonies. Unfortunately, a detachment of Raleigh's men attacked a Spanish settlement on Venezuela's Orinoco River, violating the existing Spanish-English peace treaty—and the condition of Raleigh's pardon. On his return to England, Raleigh became something of a sacrificial lamb. He was rearrested and, at least in part to placate the Spanish ambassador, Sir Walter Raleigh was beheaded at the Tower in October 1618.

It is somewhat ironic. For all his efforts, Sir Walter never did discover that legendary source of New World gold and silver. In fact, what he is probably best known for today is the popularization of tobacco. Raleigh never set foot on North America, either, but Virginia tobacco became the "brown gold" of the first English colony for the next two hundred years.

England for assistance. During his absence, full-blown war with Spain broke out, fought largely at sea. Every English ship was engaged in the conflict, which included, of course, the famed English defeat of the Spanish Armada in 1588.

It was three years before White finally was able to return to Roanoke Island with resupplies in August 1590. When he arrived, the colony of 115 people had vanished without a trace or sign of struggle, its houses and palisades dismantled in seemingly organized fashion. The only clue was a single word, "Croatoan," carved on a post of the wooden stockade—the name of an island and its Indian inhabitants some fifty miles to the south.

Countless theories have been advanced by historians and archaeologists over the years, some more plausible than others, but no definitive explanation has been advanced and accepted for the colony's disappearance. The mystery of the lost colony of Roanoke Island remains. The island

Leased by the Queen to Sir Walter in 1592, twelfth-century Sherborne Castle proved a little rustic for the courtier and his ambitions. So, Raleigh built a "lodge" in the field next door that became Sherborne New Castle. There were times over the next few years when he had to retreat to the Dorset countryside and keep his head down.

today stands in Dare County, North Carolina, named after the babe who was born there in 1587.

ENDGAME FOR THE TUDOR DYNASTY

When the childless Queen Elizabeth died in 1601 after forty-three years on the throne of England, her heir was indeed the son of her cousin, Mary, now King James VI of Scotland. And James had been waiting for this. The Tudor dynasty begun on Bosworth Field was over. The fate of the united crown of England and Scotland, now Great Britain, was in the hands of the Royal Stuarts. Surrounded by sycophants and servants, King James made a triumphal progress south, the 480 miles from Edinburgh to London—and never returned to his northern kingdom again.

From the very beginning, the new King James I of England clashed with the English Parliament and his leading nobles. Parliament was not a new institution in London. The English monarch had been reigning with a Parliament for three hundred years. That the king was subject to law had been fought out with King John and his successors back in the 1200s beginning with Magna Carta's provisions sealed at Runnymede in 1215 by an admittedly coerced King John. In fact, the first representative Parliament had been called in 1255 by Simon de Montfort, the Earl of Leicester, who was effectively regent at the time of the First Baron's War with King Henry III. The new Scottish monarchy, however, had modeled the Continental, and particularly French, notion of kingship with expectations of absolute monarchy. King James would have his royal prerogatives and his rights; God had given them to him.

In the midst of a renegade and stubbornly independent people, James found his natural allies in the old nobility and in the Episcopal hierarchy. He found his nemesis in the burghers, gentry, and yeoman of the Commons, and in the Puritans.

CHAPTER 4

Of Puritans and Pilgrims

The stars, that nature hung in heaven, and filled their lamps with everlasting oil, give due light to the misled and lonely traveler.
—John Milton

Creeping Puritan Influence Takes Its Toll

Intellectual historians claim that it generally takes three generations for worldview-shaking ideas to get from their origination to common currency in the marketplace of ideas. By the time James VI took the High Road to London to become King James I of England, the Reformation theology and the fervor it engendered that became the Puritan movement was in its second generation. For twenty years or more now, the university at Cambridge, particularly Emmanuel College, had been a center of this new Protestant thought.

Every element of church belief and practice was new, from how the church should be decorated (or not decorated, as it happens) to the liturgy and celebration of worship, to the very organization of the ecclesiastical hierarchy. It seemed that everything was challenged—especially the church's long-assumed control over the individual's soul. From Cambridge, young clerics went out into the parishes of the Eastern Counties and farther afield preaching a very different gospel from the one the villagers had been accustomed to hearing for nearly a thousand years.

Yes, Puritans wanted to strip the churches of their icons, relics, saints, and other vestiges of Catholic devotion. For Protestants, the central focus of worship was the preaching and teaching of the word of God, rather

Emmanuel was founded in 1584 by Queen Elizabeth's Chancellor of the Exchequer, Sir Walter Mildmay, for the schooling of Puritan pastors. Among the college's many graduates who ultimately emigrated to Massachusetts Bay was John Harvard. Harvard University was modeled on Emmanuel College.

than the celebration of the Eucharist. Among the lessons those Puritan preachers taught was that every individual was equal before God, and responsible for their own relationship with God. There was no spiritual hierarchy that led from their lowly humble selves through to the priest and on up the Episcopal chain of command: Peasant, priest and Pope, burgher and bishop were equal before God. Almost as startling, so were bailiff and baron, pauper and peer of the realm.

If all are equal before God, then the worth of the individual does not depend upon the accident of their parentage.

This was revolutionary stuff. With that personal responsibility before God, the idea that every believer in Jesus Christ was his or her own priest, came the equally contentious notion that not only should the Bible be available in the English vernacular of the people, but that everyone should become literate in order to be able to read and study the Word of God for themselves.

What the young Puritan pastors took into the English parish churches was not simply some denominational adjustments in faith and practice, but an entirely new, mind-blowing worldview. The reception with which this radical and even alarming new Protestant gospel was greeted was understandably mixed, but as the Puritan message spread, the results resonated far beyond the devotional.

From time immemorial, people had accepted a hierarchical world. Every sentient creature in God's creation had the place into which it was born. Human beings had their place in the hierarchy as well, born into peasantry or nobility according to God's ordination. German philosopher Gottfried Leibniz called it "the great chain of being." That hierarchical existence was reflected in the spiritual hierarchy as well. Challenging the clerics and spiritual lords above one was as unthinkable as challenging the bailiff and the temporal lords who held feudal sway over physical life.

If, however, we are all equal before God, then there is really no such thing as a "spiritual lord." As in Tennyson's "Lady of Shalott," the mirror cracked from side to side—or the great chain of being lost its links. If all are equal before God, then the worth of the individual does not depend upon the accident of their parentage. The Puritan gospel not only challenged religious practice, it undermined the very foundations of society. It certainly threatened King James I, his old-blood nobility, and the English bishops.

If "the Establishment" was threatened by the implied and intrinsic egalitarianism of the Reformation message, however, it was exciting, water in the desert out in the provinces. For the first time, people could nourish rather than quell a sense of aspiration.

Perhaps the group of people for whom the new Puritan gospel held the most appeal was the small middling class of Englishmen who were the gentry and the mercantile folk. The gentry were hardly the hereditary barons and titled peers, the feudal tenants-in-chief who carved up counties between them. They were freeholders, the "Lords of the Manor"

As late as 1848, in her *Hymns for Little Children*, hymnodist Cecil Frances Alexander's "All Things Bright and Beautiful" included the following original third stanza.

"The rich man in his castle,
The poor man at his gate,
God made them high and lowly
And ordered each estate."

whose holdings were a village or two, who farmed the "home farm," lived in the manor house, paid for the support of the parish church, and read the new Geneva Bible. The burghers in London, Norwich, Bristol, and the port towns were the merchants who made good income moving and trading wool to the continent, importing goods and equipping ships.

These were the men that made up the House of Commons. They had no vested interest in the old oligarchic power structure of church and state. In the message of the Puritan Reformation, they found a confirmation of their worth as individuals and support for their own spiritual and temporal aspirations. This was a class that had the means and education to provide fertile topsoil for the seeds being cast. And this was the standing to which tradesmen, craftsmen, and ambitious families by hard work and education could aspire.

THE MILLENARY PETITION AND ITS AFTERMATH

On King James's way to London, he was presented with a petition signed by a thousand Puritan clergymen from across England detailing their objections to the Romanist practices of the Anglican Church. The king summoned a parley at Hampton Court Palace in January 1604; what is known as the Millenary Petition was deliberated. The list of petitions presented by the Puritan divines would have substantially stripped the Church of England of its Anglo-Catholic roots and created a firmly Reformed model of worship and doctrine.

With the counsel of his leading (politically supportive, aristocratic) Anglo-Catholic churchmen, King James denied all the petitioners' requests—save one. The king agreed that the English church should have a uniform, properly authorized English translation of the Bible. In consequence, teams of scholars were set up at Oxford, Cambridge, and Westminster to render the oldest available manuscripts (the *Textus Receptous* or "received text") of the Bible into the commonly spoken English vernacular of the day. Their result was the publication in 1611 of the Authorized Version of the Bible. What quickly became known as the King James Version became the "official" Bible and the pulpit Bible in Anglican churches from Newquay to Newcastle. It also went on to become what is still the bestselling book of all time.

Beyond the undeniably world-changing decision that resulted in the King James Bible, the Hampton Court Conference was a complete bust for the Puritans. Not only did the king reject outright all the ecclesiastical and doctrinal substance of their grievance and their spiritual passion, but the conference hardened his resolve and opposition to everything the Puritan clerics represented. There was another pragmatic result.

King James's Bible

The 1611 Authorized Version of the Bible coming out of the 1604 Hampton Court Conference with the king's blessing was produced in translation by forty-seven church scholars working in teams at Westminster Abbey and the Universities of Oxford and Cambridge. It supplanted the Bishops' Bible in Church of England pulpits and, in 1633, the Geneva Bible in Scotland. By the early 1700s the version had become universally adopted by English-language Protestant churches, a dominance it maintained until newer versions emerged in the twentieth century—though the KJV still remains widely used in Protestant churches and widely read.

While no accurate figures can reveal how many copies of the King James Version have been printed and distributed over the centuries, the Bible Society's attempt to calculate it estimated that nearly six billion copies had been put into circulation by 1992.

Over the next couple of years, some three hundred of the most obdurate Puritan vicars were removed from their livings and their churches by the Chancery Court. Among those was Richard Clyfton, rector of All Saints Church in the village of Babworth on the western edge of Nottinghamshire, who was suspended in 1605. His congregation left the church with him. From early 1606, Clyfton's congregation of Calvinist Dissenters met for worship a few miles east on the route of the Great North Road (today's A1) in the nearby village of Scrooby at the ancestral manor home of the local gentry, William Brewster.

Brewster had attended Peterhouse College, Cambridge, and in 1584 entered the service of William Davison, Queen Elizabeth I's secretary of state. He served as diplomatic adjutant to Davison on several missions to the Netherlands. When Davison fell from favor, Brewster returned to Scrooby Manor and took his father's position as regional postmaster and bailiff for the Archbishop of York. In both Cambridge

Just up the street from Scrooby Manor and the parish church, Scrooby's village pub, the appropriately named Pilgrim Fathers, tells much of the local story in artifacts and replicas.

and the Netherlands, Brewster absorbed Reformed theology and the Congregational ethos. When Clyfton and his parishioners abandoned Babworth church in 1605, Brewster invited them to gather at Scrooby Manor—right across the street from St. Wilfrid's village church, where Brewster himself was baptized and had regularly worshipped. In private hands today, part of the Elizabethan farmhouse of Scrooby Manor still stands.

In the larger market town of Gainsborough, a dozen miles east and just over the Lincolnshire border, a Separatist group had been meeting at Gainsborough Old Hall at the invitation of its owner, Sir William Hickman. Their pastor was John Smythe, deposed by the Bishop of Lincoln from his Lincoln church, who had come to Gainsborough in 1603. His congregation of some seventy souls came from villages throughout a fifteen-mile radius. When Brewster invited Clyfton to Scrooby Manor, those from Scrooby and several eastern villages joined the religious refugees from Babworth. Among them was a young William Bradford of Austerfield. Austerfield's village bistro, The Mayflower, commemorates the birthplace of Pilgrim leader William Bradford, a generation younger than Brewster.

We are all, in all places, strangers and pilgrims —*William Bradford*

Meanwhile, just a few miles to the southwest in Sturton la Steeple, John Robinson had also lost his church because of his Puritan convictions. Many of his congregation merged with the Gainsborough Separatists. Subsequently, Robinson himself assumed the office of teacher of the Scrooby congregation; Richard Clyfton remained preacher; William Brewster the lay elder. Puritan Dissenters had become Congregational Separatists.

Under the dictates of King James I, it was illegal not to attend regularly the local established Church of England. William Brewster's own refusal to worship with the Anglican Church was bound to attract attention. He was the only one of the Pilgrims who had a diplomatic and political background. Brewster lost his job as postmaster. He and others were imprisoned and fined in York. Families were spied upon and their homes raided. Others lost their livelihoods. At both Scrooby and Gainsborough, the Separatists made plans to leave England and began to sell their belongings.

In 1607 the congregation in Scrooby made an attempt to flee the hostile environment, to find a new life with the Dutch Reformed saints in the Netherlands. Their attempted escape via ship from the Lincolnshire coast was betrayed—there's a monument on Fishtoft Creek commemorating their interception. Leaders, including Brewster, Clyfton, and Bradford, were briefly imprisoned in the Guildhall jail cells in the port town of Boston, and their friends and dejected followers sent back to their villages. Both the Pilgrim families and their leaders reported of their kind and gracious treatment during their detention in Boston. Despite the acts of officialdom, Boston's townspeople were strongly Puritan, and sympathetic to the Pilgrims' plight. Those Guildhall cells still stand in what is now Boston's local history museum.

The next year the Scrooby church family tried again, and this time they succeeded in leaving England behind them for the hospitable climes of Protestant Holland. In early 1608, Smythe and some forty of the Gainsborough congregation simply disappeared. It is not known how they got there, but the group emerged in Amsterdam and joined a community of three hundred English Separatist émigrés in that city, where the Dutch Reformed Church was accepting and supportive.

When the Scrooby folk led by Brewster, Robinson, and Clyfton made their successful flight later in the year, they landed first in Amsterdam and were welcomed by the expat community. To maintain their own faith community and congregation, they ultimately settled twenty-five miles south in the city of Leiden. Once the congregation of roughly a hundred arrived in Leiden, they elected William Brewster as their ruling elder. Over the next decade, Brewster taught English at the University of Leiden and published religious tracts. Many of the group were weavers and worked at the looms producing wool, linen, and fustian cloth. Life was not easy.

THEY WERE NOT ALONE

Meanwhile, King James and the bishops dug in their silver spurs. That natural alliance between James and the old nobility just as naturally included the upper echelons of the Church of England. The movers and shakers of that church had always been part of that interrelated family.

We are accustomed to thinking of the leadership hierarchy of any institution or organization as being something of a meritocracy. If someone is the colonel of a regiment or the vice chairman of the board, we assume that the position is earned by experience and merit. That whole notion, though, is a relatively new concept in human relations. In the seventeenth century (and for much of previous recorded history) the accepted leadership hierarchy of society, both secular and ecclesiastical, was determined by blood and birth rather than such intangibles as knowledge, competence, and leadership ability.

In short, the bishops of England and church leaders above and below them in ecclesiastical rank most often came from the same old aristocratic families loyal to King James. By the age-old common law of primogeniture, the oldest son inherited the land and the title; for ambitious younger sons, the Church was the most propitious avenue to power. It was also an effective means to expand the family's influence and importance.

Increasingly through the early 1600s, at the parish level the churches and both their clerical and lay leadership were theologically Reformed—Puritan with the enthusiasm of newly made converts. At the level of institutional power, though, the Church remained firmly Anglo-Catholic, relishing the trappings of authority such as their ecclesiastical dress and the rituals of liturgical worship. And thus they were natural allies of the king, by family blood loyalties and class instinct, as well as religion.

CHAPTER 5

Beginnings of Migration: The Plantation of Virginia

A great emigration necessarily implies unhappiness of some kind or other in the country that is deserted.

—THOMAS MALTHUS

MUCH OF OUR STORY FOR THE NEXT CENTURY AND A HALF IS A TALE OF migration. What became eventually thirteen colonies were all populated principally with an ongoing stream of people uprooting their lives in Britain and, leaving all behind, taking a dangerous sail of six to eight weeks across the North Atlantic—with deteriorating rations and no privacy—into an unknown, dangerous New World.

The circumstances were so different from one colony to another, from one set of planners, dreamers, and families to those in the colony down the coast or up the river. It is quite amazing how our narrative unravels as the colonies grow into a common cause and forge together an entirely new concept of nationhood in the 1770s.

AMERICA'S FOUNDING CHAMPION AND THE VIRGINIA COMPANY

By the time the *Mayflower* Pilgrims landed near Cape Cod a dozen years after their voluntary exile to the Netherlands, however, they would not be the first. The North Atlantic coast had been actively explored and probed for years. By that time, there was a French settlement on the St. Lawrence River, and a struggling English colony on a peninsula in Chesapeake Bay.

41

Among the intrepid explorers of the North Atlantic in the years of Queen Elizabeth was one Bartholomew Gosnold. Born into a reasonably prominent gentry family on the border of Essex and Suffolk in 1572 and schooled with his cousins at the family seat of Otley Hall, Gosnold took to cartography and navigation. Gosnold went on to Cambridge and subsequently trained in law at Middle Temple. Probably inspired by the travel accounts of Richard Hakylet, the New World captured Gosnold's imagination.

British expeditions across the Atlantic had been ongoing from the 1570s, with each successful return adding to the store of New World knowledge and fueling the imagination of others. Bartholomew Gosnold made his first voyage across with one of the most active champions of exploration and colonization, Sir Walter Raleigh. A number of temporary camps and settlements were attempted along the Atlantic coast. Most famously, of course, there was Raleigh's lost mystery colony at Roanoke Island in 1587, but he was not alone in the dream.

In several voyages of exploration across the Atlantic over the next few years, Bartholomew Gosnold charted the entire coast of Newfoundland. Then, with Raleigh's backing, Gosnold led his own attempt to begin a colony in 1602. In command of the *Concord*, with only twenty colonists aboard, Gosnold took a more northerly Atlantic crossing than was customary in those early days, and made landfall at Cape Elizabeth, near what is now Portland, Maine.

Sailing south along the coast, Gosnold discovered and named the promontory of Cape Cod. Off its southern coast, he named one of the islands after his recently deceased daughter and from the abundance of wild grapes: Martha's Vineyard. The group landed south of the Cape on what is now Cuttyhunk Island—protected from the northern weather and naturally defended against any threat by a hostile indigenous people. They chivalrously named it Elizabeth Island.

Intending to build a settlement, the nascent colonists spent several weeks planning and working on a stockade. Apparently Gosnold and the colonists realized, however, that they were not adequately prepared and supplied for the long, frigid winter to come. Undoubtedly with some reluctance, the decision was made to abandon the colony and return to

Early Profit on the New England Coast

Bartholomew Gosnold was hardly the only explorer along the New England coastline. On Route 1 along midcoast Maine at the southern edge of Penobscot Bay, road signs welcoming visitors to the town of Thomaston bear the year 1605. Few people question that, though obviously Thomaston's settlement does not date from then.

In June 1605, however, explorer Captain George Weymouth (or Waymouth) on the ship *Archangel* sailed up the estuary of the St. Georges River and anchored at a natural haven along the jagged coast. While Weymouth and his crew explored the area, they discovered mature stands of tall, straight trees ideal for ships' masts—a rich prize indeed. Felling trees enough to fill his ship, they returned to England with their valuable cargo. For more than a century English ships made the voyage up the St. Georges River to harvest masts and hardwoods for shipbuilding, the first "cash crop" of the New World. To this day, in many towns along northern New England's coast and navigable rivers you can find a Mast Road.

Thomaston itself became a center of shipbuilding. At the town landing today stands the Weymouth Cross commemorating Captain Weymouth's landing and the birth of New England's earliest industry.

England before the winter made the Atlantic crossing impossibly treacherous. They loaded up the *Concord* with skins and furs and sailed home. Bartholomew Gosnold's first dream of an English colony in America had ended in failure.

Try, Try Again

Bartholomew Gosnold was a visionary for his time and remained convinced that a permanent settlement in the land that England knew then as Virginia could be, among other things, profitable. Bartholomew Gosnold was not about to give up. Through the early years of King James I's reign, Gosnold became a key figure in the organization of the Virginia

Company. Many planning meetings were held at the Gosnold seat of Otley Hall near Ipswich. Apparently, during those years, William Shakespeare was a common visitor; local legend has it that *A Midsummer Night's Dream* was first staged at Otley.

Gosnold's experience at Elizabeth Island had taught him that much more elaborate preparation was necessary for success. He also determined that a viable colony should be attempted farther south than rugged and seemingly inhospitable New England with its harsh winters.

The Virginia Company was a stock company, funded largely by London merchants. Its purpose was to establish a profitable plantation, shipping fish, lumber, pelts, and hopefully gold back to the English market. Gosnold wanted entrepreneurs, and that's what he got: gentlemen with cash to invest. Ready to launch the venture, the company received its charter from James I in April 1606. A party of 144 sailors and colonists sailed that December in three ships under the command of Christopher Newport, *Susan B. Constant*, *Godspeed*, and *Discovery*. Gosnold captained the *Godspeed* as second-in-command.

The small flotilla was waylaid by storms and stops along its southern route via the Caribbean, but reached the mouth of Chesapeake Bay at Hampton Roads in April 1607. Turning into Chesapeake Bay, they at last landed on a peninsula almost fifty miles up the James River, where a deepwater anchorage made water access easy. The Virginia Company had settled Jamestown.

Their royal charter stipulated that the Virginia Company colony was to be governed by a seven-man appointed council. To preserve maritime command during the voyage, the names of those appointed were sealed, not to be opened until the company reached land. When the council was revealed, Gosnold's name was at the top of the list. That body elected Gosnold's cousin Edward Wingfield its president. Wingfield proved unsuitable and short-lived; however, no leadership could have made a success that summer.

It was a disastrous venture in almost every respect. The choice of location where the colonists began constructing a stockade and housing could not have been more poorly advised.

It is difficult to imagine today how the swampy land abutting the palisades of Jamestown would render a community habitable at all without the modern "conveniences" of pesticides and air-conditioning.

Occupying what is known today as Jamestown Island, with a narrow isthmus to the mainland that at that time flooded with the tide, the settlement's positioning was thought to be strong, because of its defensibility against any hostile natives and because of its six-fathom anchorage. Built on low, marshy ground and fetid wetlands, though, the colony was indefensible against attack of another kind. The Virginia Tidewater was plagued with mosquitoes and sundry insects and a veritable incubator of disease.

Built on low, marshy ground and fetid wetlands, the colony was indefensible against attack of another kind.

The colonists themselves were hardly equipped for the adventure. Virtually all of them were male, most in their teens and early twenties. The oldest among them were in their early thirties. Of the 105 settlers on the manifest, 59 listed themselves as "Gentleman."

Whether they were investors, adventurers, or scoundrels, gentlemen did not work. Most of the remaining colonists were indentured servants: indentured to the gentlemen. They were expected to do all the actual physical labor. When summer heat hits the Virginia Tidewater, temperatures are in the nineties for weeks at a time, with tropical humidity. Men who had grown up laboring in summer temperatures of the sixties and low seventies with little humidity simply couldn't work effectively in that climate.

Fevers and dysentery, poor diet, fetid water, and brutal climate conditions quickly took a serious toll on the colony. Almost half of the settlers, fifty of them, died of the accumulated conditions that first summer—including Bartholomew Gosnold, on August 22.

Presumed to be the burial place of Bartholomew Gosnold, the grave was discovered in 2003 by Preservation Virginia archaeologists. Its coffin, decorated with a captain's staff, contained an intact skeleton of appropriate age. Efforts to positively identify the remains by DNA testing failed when the grave of Gosnold's sister back in England proved not to contain his sister.

Most of the men dying in Jamestown that year were interred within the palisades of the fortress, to mask from the local Indians the company's rapidly declining strength. Gosnold, however, was buried outside the stockade, with full honors accorded to his leadership and rank. His prominence was considered such that his disappearance would be noted by the natives in any event. Ultimately, leadership of the Jamestown colony devolved to the man much better known to history, John Smith, and Bartholomew Gosnold was largely forgotten.

The Jamestown colonists nearly gave up and determined to return to England before a relief ship arrived in the autumn of 1607. For several years, the colony struggled merely to exist, taking a huge percentage of the lives cast to its fate.

John Smith's own history as an early Jamestown leader is checkered to say the least. He was about twenty-eight when he joined the Jamestown expedition, already an experienced mercenary soldier fighting the Spaniards and the Ottoman Turks. Allegedly charged with mutiny on the voyage and nearly hanged, Smith arrived at Jamestown Island in chains. As he had been named one of the colony's governing council, Smith was released from custody after a few weeks, and was eventually given charge of bartering with the local native Indians for food. Partly in search of food, in the summer of 1608, Smith set out to explore and roughly chart what was the entire coastline of Chesapeake Bay, covering some three thousand miles. He became president of Jamestown's governing council in September 1608. When a summer drought that year led to food scarcity, the native tribes refused to sell rations to the colonists. Smith simply took the wanted food, waging attacks and burning villages, in some cases imprisoning and forcing Indians into labor.

In 1609 John Smith was badly injured in a gunpowder explosion, and the Virginia Company drafted a new colonial charter. Smith gave up his leadership in Jamestown and returned to England that summer, expected to answer charges of misconduct for his dealings with the Indians. They seem to have been forgotten. Smith himself was determined not to be. He published an account on Virginia, its native indigenous tribes, topography, climate, vegetation, and wildlife.

The winter of 1609 in Jamestown became known as the "Starving Time," taking all but a fraction of the settlers by starvation and privation. Lord De La Warr arrived the next spring with a fleet of supplies and newly recruited settlers as the first royal governor of Virginia.

Smith returned to North America on a voyage of mercantile adventure and exploration in 1614 along the coast of Maine and Massachusetts Bay. While Smith intended to return with a cargo of whale oil, he brought back to England a boatload of beaver furs. In the process, he became the first Englishman to set foot on and chart the Isles of Shoals. A monument to Smith stands on Star Island, New Hampshire. Of course, Smith had named them Smith's Isles. He also first named the region New England and gave place-names to a number of features along the coast.

Despite several attempts, Smith never returned to Virginia or to the New England coast. He published accounts of his adventures in both regions, and valuable maps of their coastlines. Unhappily, John Smith was prone to grandiose self-promotion, known for embroidering his own exploits and creating texts of debatable reliability. Happily for Smith, at least, he dined out on tales of his adventures the rest of his life in England and died in 1631.

Certainly the most famous story of Virginia's early years is the far more romantic account of Princess Pocahontas, the daughter of tribal Indian chieftain Powhatan. In legend, at least, the teenage girl had saved John Smith's neck by urging her father Powhatan not to kill him. During

A Few Years Later . . .

When the *Mayflower* Pilgrims finally settled on the place where they would set foot on Plymouth Rock, it already had a place-name. It is popular supposition that the Pilgrim congregation named their new home Plymouth after their last port of call in England—Plymouth. In fact, that stretch near the elbow of Cape Cod had already been named Plymouth on John Smith's 1614 map. That just happened to be where the Pilgrims landed and built their plantation.

On the south bank of the River Thames near its estuary at the English Channel, the statue of the Indian princess standing in the Pocahontas Garden is a replica of her commemorative statue in Jamestown.

Indian hostilities in 1613, she was captured by the colonists for ransom. As it happens, she converted to Christianity and chose to stay with the settlers. Pocahontas took the name of Rebecca and famously married farmer John Rolfe. They traveled to London in 1616, where she was feted by society, presented at court, and generally shown off to promote trade and settlement in Virginia. In something of a bitter irony, while they were preparing to return home to Jamestown, Pocahontas contracted the plague and died in March 1617 at the age of twenty-two. She is buried with a memorial statue and garden at St. George's Church, Gravesend.

In 1622 an attack by native Indians to repay an assumed grudge left 350 colonists dead. Bit by bit, though, the persistent colony of Virginia established a foothold along the peninsula between the James River and the York River, then farther afield to the north and south, building plantation settlements and beginning to produce cash crops—in particular tobacco. It would be forty years, however, before Virginia reached a population of eight thousand and the sustainability of the colony was assured.

TOBACCO: THE MAKING OF THE SOUTH

Tobacco had been around a long time. Columbus was offered it down in the Caribbean during his first, 1492, voyage. Explorers and merchant adventurers from Portugal, Spain, and France had brought the pungent, addictive herb back to Europe through the 1500s. It was apparently brought back the first time to England on one of Sir Walter Raleigh's sponsored New World sails to Carolina and Roanoke Island. The smoking of tobacco was quickly found to be enjoyable—and medicinal.

Colonists in Jamestown early on discovered that tobacco was cultivated by the region's Powhatan Indians, both for their own use and as a medium of trade and exchange. The English settlers soon grew tobacco for use as a local currency. Ships bringing immigrants and supplies willingly carried back to England a cargo of tobacco to a ready and ever-expanding market. It was tobacco that made John Rolfe the first wealthy farmer in Jamestown and enabled him to take his Indian princess bride to England. Virginia had quickly discovered a cash crop that was highly profitable—enough to create a new agrarian economy, determine a way of life, and in the coming decades propel the colony to prosperity.

The nitrogen-rich, fertile soil and hot, moist climate of the Chesapeake basin was ideal for growing the high-quality and highly prized "Virginia" tobacco. But its cultivation, planting, curing, and preparation for market were labor intensive. Plantation owners soon found that indentured servants (promised freedom and land at the end of their indenture) were not going to be an efficient, sustainable source of labor. The economic advantages as well as the planters' hierarchical worldview led toward the African race slavery that drove the economy of Virginia and later the Carolinas for two hundred years until the War between the States.

Unraveling History in Jamestown: Sir George Yeardly

Ongoing archeological excavations in Jamestown are carried out by the Jamestown Rediscovery Foundation. In the summer of 2018, a major discovery was uncovered in the chancel of the standing brick church built in 1617 that called attention to one of colonial history's most important forgotten leaders.

Sir George Yeardly, son of a London tailor, arrived in Jamestown in 1610 as a young soldier. By 1616 he was the colony's governor, returning to England the next year. In 1618 he was appointed governor of Virginia again and knighted by King James I. He returned to Jamestown charged by the Virginia Company with establishing a "laudable form of government . . . for the people there inhabiting" and uniting the spreading regional settlements to "one body corporate, and live under equal and like law."

Yeardly sent word ahead, charging each small community to send two delegates to a conclave in Jamestown. In 1619 thirty men gathered on the site of the same brick church; it was the first representative legislative assembly in the New World. Perhaps ironically, that same year brought the first enslaved Africans to the colony, and Yeardly became one of the first slaveholders.

Sir George Yeardly died in 1627 during his third term as colonial governor. The grave discovered lies in the middle aisle of the church just in front of the altar, a fitting place for the "state burial" of a governor and a knight.

The fashion of smoking and otherwise using tobacco spread across England (and Continental Europe) through the seventeenth century. Its use was hailed by doctors and scientists as a super medicine, good for preserving health and curing headaches and fatigue. As immigration to Virginia by Royalist aristocrats increased through the mid-1600s, new plantations sprang up, knowing their business and their profitable cash crop from the beginning. It created a powerful enticement for the building of the Virginia colony and the making of fortunes.

MEANWHILE, FRANCE TOO CLAIMS A STAKE

It seems almost parenthetical to the narrative that Americans learn of our earliest days of colonial settlement, but England was not the only European power interested in the new North Atlantic world. In 1534 King Francis I commissioned mariner Jacques Cartier on a voyage of exploration to North America. Cartier skirted Newfoundland, found Prince Edward Island, and explored the Gulf of St. Lawrence, claiming his discovered territory for France. On subsequent trips over the next half dozen years, Cartier sailed the St. Lawrence, wintered over in Quebec twice, and got as far inland as Montreal, where river rapids prevented easy navigation farther upriver.

Navigable to the Great Lakes, the St. Lawrence gave French explorers, traders, missionary priests, and settlers unfettered access deep into the continent.

The motivation of Cartier's expeditions was not simply intellectual curiosity or even a desire for lands to claim as such. Rich mineral prizes of copper, silver, and gold, highly valued spices, and a water route to Asia (the elusive Northwest Passage) were the goals. Reports of the native Indians encouraged Cartier to believe that they were there. The unexpected severity of the northern winters and the decided lack of any worthwhile materials findings, however, led the king to abandon the ventures in 1541. France had claimed the land, but virtually ignored North America for more than fifty years.

It was in the summer following Jamestown's settlement, in 1608, that Samuel de Champlain brought a group of French settlers to establish the first permanent French community in the New World. They located at what is now Quebec City. Strategically situated on the St. Lawrence River, Quebec ultimately gave the French control over access to interior Canada and the Great Lakes.

The following year, 1609, Champlain discovered the lake that bears his name, now forming the northern part of the New York–Vermont border. More significantly, Champlain made an alliance with the Huron and Algonquin Indians in their hostilities with the Iroquois. Subsequently, that alliance eventually drove the Iroquois to side with the English.

The early French settlement in Canada was a thousand miles by sea (and an unknown continent away by land) from the English colony in Virginia. French occupation of Atlantic Canada, just a year after the first English settlers landed in Virginia (and a dozen years before the Pilgrims claimed Plymouth Rock), however, set the stage for a major motif in the English colonies' development for 150 years.

France's highway into the New World was the St. Lawrence River. Flowing northeast from Lake Ontario, the river drains large parts of the Upper Midwest, the Adirondacks, Ontario, and Quebec before broadening into the Gulf of St. Lawrence some nineteen hundred miles from its headwaters in Minnesota's Mesabi Range. Navigable to the Great Lakes, the St. Lawrence gave French explorers, traders, missionary priests, and settlers unfettered access deep into the continent. From the beginning, France had a stake in the New World, and an open river road into its interior.

CHAPTER 6

The Exodus to Massachusetts

Thus out of small beginnings greater things have been produced by His hand that made all things of nothing and gives being to all things that are; and as one small candle may light a thousand; so the light here kindled hath shone unto many, yea in some sort to our whole nation; let the glorious name of Jehovah have all the praise.
— GOVERNOR WILLIAM BRADFORD

KING JAMES'S PROBLEMS JUST MULTIPLY

Back in England, the stubborn Stuart monarch was increasingly coming into conflict with his House of Commons. The English Parliament was accustomed to being consulted, and they held the purse strings. The king had plenty of income from his own estates and from various traditional grants and customs that served principally to operate the court and maintain a royal standard of living in the context of the times.

What the royal purse could not do, however, was raise taxes and finance wars. For that, for taxes and grants of money, the monarch was dependent upon a Parliament that was increasingly Puritan. Its newfound sense of identity in the Reformation worldview inclined the Commons to be increasingly bent on showing its political muscle.

King James's prime ambition was to maintain the "royal prerogative," to practice his kingship by demonstrating his authority and jealously guarding both authority and power. Once again, this was the attitude toward absolute monarchy that the Stuarts had picked up largely by their close alliance with the French monarchy for generations. James spent money profligately and doled out peerages cheaply to his friends.

Like almost every monarch, of course, sooner or later King James needed to raise taxes from a Parliament. In this case, the Parliament elected was made recalcitrant by his hostility to their Reformed faith and its practice, and by their insistence that the Commons had a rightful role in the nation's governance. Having found his natural alliance in the English Church hierarchy, James was quick enough to abandon any kind of allegiance to the Presbyterianism in which he was raised in favor of the High Church of England.

FROM LEIDEN TO THE NEW WORLD

The dissenting Scrooby congregation that made its way from Nottinghamshire and Lincolnshire to the Netherlands in 1608 had maintained their community. They were craftsmen and merchant families, who worked and worshipped largely among themselves and raised their families in peace with their Dutch neighbors. As the next ten years went by, however, the English settlers realized that assimilation was inevitable and that their English identity would invariably be weakened over the years as their children and grandchildren became increasingly Dutch. It was also an increasingly unwelcoming land.

Of course, the close-knit church family did not stay in the Netherlands. As a community of faith and wanting to retain their English identity, they began casting about for plan B, and settled on His Majesty's colonial possession in the New World. While some were happy to stay in their new home, in 1619 many in the congregation prepared to seek life in a new English homeland across the Atlantic.

Deacon John Carver and Robert Cushman were deputized to London to make arrangements. There, they negotiated rights with the London Company and chartered the *Mayflower* and the *Speedwell* for the famous transatlantic crossing in 1620.

In the end, only thirty-five members of the original Separatist exiles were aboard the *Mayflower* by the time it sailed. John Robinson remained in Leiden to pastor the larger group remaining. He died in 1625. Over the next few years, however, many of those left in Leiden joined their friends and families in Plymouth Colony, and the English community in the Netherlands gradually disappeared.

Richard Clyfton was an old man when the group landed in the Netherlands. He remained in Amsterdam and died in 1616. *Mayflower* sailed with John Carver as the appointed governor of the new settlement and William Brewster the ruling elder. Also aboard was William Bradford, who became a leader in the New World colony for thirty years, governor and author of *Of Plymouth Plantation*. The phrase in Robert Cushman's Bible is attributed to Bradford:

"We are all, in all places, strangers and pilgrims"

Here the story becomes well known. The congregation that we know as the Pilgrims laid their plans, chartered the *Mayflower* and the *Speedwell*, and left Leiden for England and, ultimately, with stops in London, Southampton, and Plymouth (where there are memorials in each city), an Atlantic crossing to a new life.

The *Speedwell* proving unseaworthy, the *Mayflower* eventually set sail from Plymouth by itself. In addition to Captain Christopher Jones and crew, there were 102 passengers. The site where the Pilgrim adventurers bade their final farewell is commemorated today in Plymouth harbor by what have been known for generations as the Mayflower Steps. A memorial marks the spot, and the American flag flies next to the Union Jack.

After the expectedly arduous crossing of sixty-six days, the *Mayflower* did sight land and anchored in the hook of Cape Cod in September, near what it is now Provincetown, Massachusetts. Here, before they went ashore, the nascent American colonists signed their covenant of agreement by which their New World would be governed. Authored largely by William Bradford, the result was the Mayflower Compact. It might be called the world's first charter of self-government—of the people, by the people, and for the people. It was probably the first instrument of self-government ever drawn up that reflected a Reformed Protestant view of the world.

Everywhere in England that the *Mayflower* put in bears a memorial to the occasion. This monument in Southampton near the West Quay commemorates the Pilgrim company's embarkation from here on August 15, 1620.

The Mayflower Compact

In the name of God Amen· We whose names are underwritten, the loyal subjects of our dread sovereign Lord King James by the grace of God, of Great Britain, France, and Ireland king, Defender of the Faith, & c.

Having undertaken, for the glory of God, and advancement of the Christian faith and honor of our King and Country, a voyage to plant the first colony in the Northern parts of Virginia do by these presents solemnly and mutually in the presence of God, and one of another, covenant, and combine ourselves together into a civil body politic; for the our better ordering, and preservation and furtherance of the ends aforesaid; and by virtue hereof, to enact, constitute, and frame such just and equal laws, ordinances, Acts, constitutions, and offices, from time to time, as shall be thought most meet and convenient for the general good of the colony: unto which we promise all due submission and obedience.

In witness whereof, we have hereunder subscribed our names at Cape Cod the 11th of November, in the year of the reign of our sovereign Lord King James of England, France, and Ireland the 18th and of Scotland the 54th. Anno Domini—1620.

It was signed by forty-one men, the women, children and servants not taking part in deliberations. The significance of the Compact is that it is the first civic "covenant." The Pilgrims and other Separatist congregations defined their church with a Covenant of and by individuals to be a church community. Here, the same kind of instrument covenants individuals into a civil community. The original of the Mayflower Compact is lost. The oldest surviving manuscript, in William Brewster's hand, resides at the Massachusetts State Library.

AT HOME IN PATUXET

The destination for the New World settlers and the *Mayflower* had been Virginia and the patent for their settlement had been actually the mouth of the Hudson River. Captain Jones, assessing the situation of his malnourished human cargo and the increasing dark and cold of autumn, declined to sail farther. Through the coming weeks, the *Mayflower* sent out scouting parties, looking for a prime location to stake their village and build their lives. As the season wore on, they found Patuxet. John Smith's map of a few years earlier had named the harbor and surrounding shoreline Plymouth.

The location, on the crescent of a broad, shallow harbor, was a large deserted village of the Wampanoag. A once-strong tribe of the Delaware nation, the Wampanoag ranged from southeastern Massachusetts and the Cape through Rhode Island. Patuxet was their largest community. Through 1616 and several years following, however, a deadly, contagious bacterial fever spread through the Indian tribes south and west along the coast from the north coast of Maine. The Wampanoag people were devastated and Patuxet was wiped out with the plague. The few survivors dispersed to other Wampanoag villages.

The Pilgrims and their fellow travelers found a deserted village, with cleared land, fields that had been tilled, plentiful spring water, and a rising hillside above a protected harbor. They made anchor and set ashore on December 21, 1620, and began to build their houses on Christmas Day.

There were substantial differences between the party of colonists that put ashore on Plymouth Rock and built Plymouth Plantation and those adventurers who had landed in the Chesapeake Tidewater some thirteen years earlier. Certainly, those we know as the Pilgrims were religious migrants, not economic adventurers. More importantly, they came as family units, not as a company of young men. They came with greater maturity and forethought.

Tellingly, the Pilgrim congregation brought an experienced military guard, and a professional soldier in Captain Miles Standish. The differences are apparent at a re-created Plimoth Plantation today. Their stockade was built on rising ground, on land clear-cut to provide unobstructed sightlines and a good view of the open water, with projecting ramparts to offer shot lines down the walls of the stockade. The strong house was built on the highest ground. That was the fort, with cannon aimed to the sea; it was also the meeting house, both for worship services of the church and business meetings of the community.

The conditions were right for the Plymouth colony to struggle to success, while the Jamestown colony spent decades just struggling to survive.

By their backgrounds, the Pilgrims were farmers and artisans; by their religion, they were Puritan: Everyone worked. The hardships were real; the death toll was high; the New England winters bitter beyond anything known back in the mother country. But the climate was far more conducive to the physical labor and hard work required to clear land, build homes, and raise crops. In short, the conditions were right for the Plymouth colony to struggle to success, while the Jamestown colony spent decades just struggling to survive. It's how the legends of the Pilgrim Fathers, Squanto, friendly Wampanoag Indians, and the first Thanksgiving have played into our national mythology in ways that the early Jamestown struggles have been largely lost beyond the mention of their existence. It was a little more human than that.

That first winter was horrific for the Plymouth settlers—an all-consuming effort to stay alive and comfort those who were dying. Winter had set in to New England when they began their shelters. There was no opportunity to lay in the only fuel supply—wood. There was no food supply apart from what might be hunted or snared from the bay. Weakened from poor diet and months belowdecks on board the crowded ship, they died from any infection or fever. By the spring, when the first dandelions offer a vitamin-rich green for the pot, the numbers had decreased by half. Only 51 of the 102 settlers survived. Not a single family unit was spared.

Captain Jones and the *Mayflower* sailed home for England; the surviving Pilgrims stayed. They were home. That spring, a Wampanoag man appeared at the colony conversant in English. This man, known to history as Squanto, introduced the settlers to the Wampanoag sachem, Massasoit, who lived nearby. Because of language, Squanto became liaison between the Plymouth colonists and the well-respected Indian leader of the depleted tribe. Massasoit was friendly, curious, and helpful to the English arrivals.

Unquestionably, the local Wampanoag taught the colonists vital survival skills needed in their New World—how to raise the "three sisters" of corn, beans, and squash and preserve them for the winter; to harvest shellfish and cure fish by drying; and to identify and locate edible flora and fauna of the coastal forest, from cranberries to game birds.

The stockaded village took completed shape that first summer. There was marriage and birth and there were reasons to celebrate and look forward to the coming winter far better prepared and stronger. The English custom of a communal harvest–home supper was a tradition of the agricultural calendar already centuries old when the community determined to have one and invite their Wampanoag neighbors to join the feast. Massasoit arrived with ninety Wampanoag men and four or five deer. It would have been as lavish a seasonal meal as nature would yield. There well may have been wild turkey on the menu that first Thanksgiving, but the center-of-the-plate attraction would have been venison.

In succeeding years, Plymouth did survive and grew slowly. It applied for and received a royal patent for southwest Massachusetts and Cape Cod. Outlying villages grew up, such as Duxbury and Taunton. The Colony of Plymouth's status as the prime New England destination, however, was short-lived. It soon found itself in the shadow of Massachusetts Bay Colony to the north.

A BUSTLING NORTH ATLANTIC COAST

In 1610 an English colony was settled on Newfoundland called Cuper's Cove. In 1616 the little fishing colony's second governor arrived, one Captain John Mason. His explorations of the island gave England its first map of Newfoundland.

Though the colony survived Mason's departure in 1621, it did not thrive. The next year, John Mason and a friend, Sir Ferdinando Gorges, received a patent for all the land that lay between the Merrimack and Kennebec rivers. In 1623 Mason sent a group led by David Thompson to settle a fishing colony at Odiorne Point, what is now Rye, New Hampshire. Mason and Gorges divided their proprietary colony at the Piscataqua River in 1629, the present-day boundary between New Hampshire and Maine.

Meanwhile, North in New France

The French had been settled in Quebec for a dozen years and were pushing inland to the west on the St. Lawrence River when the Pilgrims landed in 1620. At the time, however, Quebec had a population of only sixty—fewer than half the passengers and crew aboard the *Mayflower*.

About that same year, fisherman and farmer Abraham Martin arrived at Quebec with his wife, Marguerite, and the youngest of their nine children. Martin received a grant of land divided between the settled town on the riverfront and grazing field for his cattle on the cliff-top heights above. By the time of Martin's death in 1664, his pastureland was already being referred to as the Plains of Abraham. His family sold the plot to the Ursalines in 1667. Almost a century later, the ground became the site of the pivotal and most famous battle of the Seven Years' War.

Mason's portion became chartered as New Hampshire—the only colony (or state) named after an English county. That same year a fishing community was settled at the mouth of the Piscataqua River called Strawbery Banke.

We think of New England in the 1620s as the poor Pilgrims struggling to make a go of it in their small stockade-enclosed community at Plymouth. In fact, the coast of New England and Atlantic Canada became a beehive of activity and settlement. Despite the continuing vulnerability of the colony at Plymouth, in 1623 a group of Puritan clergy and merchants formed a "Council for New England" in London to promote further colonization of the New World by Puritan dissidents. Struggling outposts sprang up along the New England coast from Cape Ann to New Haven.

THE BOSTON CONNECTION

In 1612, five years after the Virginia Company reached Jamestown and the Scrooby congregation fled to the Netherlands, a new young Puritan rector was called to the port town of Boston, Lincolnshire, to assume the pulpit of St. Botolph's Church. One of the largest parish churches in

Among the largest parish churches in England, St. Botolph's was completed in 1390 at a time when Boston (a corruption of Botolph's Town) was one of the most important and wealthy ports in England, made prosperous on the strength of its wool trade with the Continent.

England, St. Botolph's has been known for generations as the "Boston Stump," its 272-foot lantern tower visible for miles across the flat fens in any direction.

The Rev. John Cotton was typical of the young Puritan firebrands of his day, schooled at Cambridge, and eager to advance the gospel. The new raised pulpit installed for Cotton's arrival at St. Botolph's still stands in the Boston church nave today. In due course, Cotton's preaching and leadership became well known, and his ministry widely popular. On the one hand, Cotton attracted people to locate to Boston to join his congregation. On the other hand, his Puritan populism attracted the disapproving attention of the bishops and the church hierarchy. Cotton was repeatedly brought up before the ecclesiastical courts.

At one point, Cotton was challenged by the Bishop of Lincoln, because he did not require his parishioners to kneel when receiving Holy Communion. Cotton replied, undoubtedly somewhat smugly, that the people did not kneel because there was no room for them to kneel in the church. Back then, there were no seats in the church nave. People came to church to stand—through Cotton's sometimes three-hour sermons. In the arching nave of St. Botolph's, shorn of contemporary furnishings, some thousand to twelve hundred could easily stand to receive the Lord's Supper.

By the 1620s John Cotton was among the most important Puritan clerics in England. If the Bishop of Lincoln was no fan, however, Cotton was not without influential backers, including the Earl of Lincoln and his family and a host of Lincolnshire gentry.

LONG LIVE THE KING!

King James I died in 1625, to be succeeded by his son as King Charles I. Just as King Henry VII had instilled in his sons the importance of the legitimate succession, so King James brought up his own son to regard the most important duty of the monarch as that of preserving the "royal prerogative"—the effective use of the God-given authority of kingship. As it should be easy to conclude at this point, Charles did not inherit the throne at a convenient time for this sort of conviction. The zeitgeist of the age was against him, and his own character similarly out of touch with his times and his kingdom.

King Charles filled the court with testimonies to his own magnificence. Among the most popular court entertainments were the elaborate masques performed for and with courtiers and royal performers. Written by the celebrated pens of the day such as Ben Jonson, and staged with great splendor by the likes of folk such as Sir Christopher Wren, the subtext of these expensive productions was invariably to highlight the king's majesty, authority, and divine appointment. Unfortunately, King Charles believed his own publicity.

The king doubled down on his father's recalcitrance to be answerable to any Parliament composed of mere subjects. He determined to correct the deviance of Puritans and Dissenters from the practice and discipline of the Church of England and its hierarchy. Not only was conformity to be enforced throughout England, but Charles purposed to bring Scotland into the ecclesiastical fold as well.

Church courts and regulation repeatedly harassed John Cotton and hundreds of clergymen with like convictions, their Reformed message undermined by the "political correctness" of the day. The dis-ease and increasing polarization of society led followers of Cotton in Boston and Puritans across the Lincolnshire fens and East Anglia to begin talking about emigration to the New World. It was an idea that spread through the late 1620s and received Cotton's blessing, as well as the Earl of Lincoln's crucial support.

Meanwhile, in the Stour Valley of Suffolk (a.k.a. "Constable Country"), John Winthrop, a barrister and son of the local squire, had become a rising lay voice of Puritan piety. In 1628 Winthrop published a tract arguing *Reasons for the Plantation of New England*. When the Massachusetts Bay Company formed as a joint-stock company in 1629, Winthrop invested heavily. Its compact, known as the Cambridge Agreement, established that Massachusetts Bay Company would be a mutual company owned by shareholders emigrating from England to the New World, and maintained the right to settle and trade in New England. The end result of the agreement was that the colony would be self-governing, unlike the struggling Virginia Company forced to answer to governing proprietors back in London. In October of 1629, John Winthrop was elected governor of the new colony.

The aim of the fledgling colony, as John Winthrop famously declared, was to plant a "city on a hill."

At last, the idea coalesced into a plan of action. There would be an exodus to form a colony near the existing colony of Plymouth Plantation. The Massachusetts Bay venture would be no small single-ship company determined to carve a struggling foothold on the New England coast, but an organized, purposeful social community. As months of preparation came to fruition, more than seven hundred people gathered to load onto an armada of eleven ships bound for Massachusetts Bay in the spring of 1630. Of these seven hundred pioneers and religious migrants, more than four hundred were from Boston and Cotton's own St. Botolph's Church.

The new colony carried its own council and the governor, John Winthrop. He sailed aboard the flotilla's flagship, *Arbella*, named for

Bequeathed by Annie Clarke 1944

1630. John Cotton bids farewell to his parishioners on the Arbella

The commemorative window in St. Botolph's shows Cotton and his followers left behind bidding their good-byes to the Puritan flotilla of 1630. It stands across the nave from the Cotton Chapel.

the sister of the Earl of Lincoln. Rev. John Cotton preached the sermon of farewell for the departing colonists. A stained-glass window in St. Botolph's Church commemorates the occasion to this day. The aim of the fledgling colony, as John Winthrop famously declared, was to plant a "city on a hill," as Jesus described it in the Sermon on the Mount recorded in Matthew 5.

The dream was for a community of faith: like-minded people who loved God and were called by His name, to worship and create the society according to the teachings of Scripture and the Reformed faith.

After the customary, uncomfortable voyage of a dozen weeks, the new colony landed as planned in what is now Boston Harbor. Massachusetts Bay Colony had arrived. By 1630 the coast of New England had been well scouted. Plymouth Plantation had not exactly become a booming metropolis, but it had survived intact and as a slowly growing community. After ten years, travel across the Atlantic may not have been any more comfortable, but it was not the novelty it had once been. From Maine to Long Island Sound, the coast was well explored and charted. Small communities and seasonal camps for fishing and logging were being established every year.

Now the arrival of seven hundred settlers at a chosen location, where the Charles River empties into Boston Harbor, was critical mass. This was the arrival, not of a village, but of a full-blown market town—complete with all the skills, crafts, and trades. Blacksmith and cobbler, farmer and sawyer, merchant, tanner, cabinetmaker, and weaver: The Puritans were a people of occupations, industry, and families. Most expected to clear and live off the land. After all, apart from the motivating freedom to worship and practice their faith as they choose, the fundamental attraction of New England was the opportunity to become freeholders—to own their own land.

The New World venture of these settlers, however, was not principally about social and economic advancement; they were on a mission. As Winthrop affirmed, "We are entered into a covenant with Him for this work." Their communal goal was to establish a land free for the exercise of true religion.

The Puritan colonists settled the promontory above the Charles River that became Boston, and set about building their "city on a hill." While their story was not without hardship, their community was large enough and strong enough to be successful, and quickly to attract others back in England to join them. The fledgling colony soon spread out into villages surrounding Massachusetts Bay—Dorchester, Charlestown, and north to Ipswich, Salem (first settled as a fishing camp in 1626 and a permanent settlement in 1629), and Newbury.

The Salem Covenant of 1629

"We covenant with the Lord and one with another, and do bind our selves in the presence of God, to walk together in all His ways, according as he is pleased to reveal Himself unto us in his blessed Word of truth."

The simple Salem Covenant became an influential statement that served as a model for many Congregational churches ordered in the fledgling New England communities established along the coast in the seventeenth century.

CHAPTER 7

New England's Great Migration

If I have seen further than others, it is by standing on the shoulders of giants

—ISAAC NEWTON

THE 1630s PURITAN FLIGHT

The 1630s were a booming decade of Puritan exodus to Massachusetts Bay. As tensions between Parliament and King Charles continued, word spread of the godly communities and rich opportunities for a new life in New England. Agents helped potential colonists prepare for the Atlantic journey and for building life on the other side, publishing supply and equipment lists. Though records are incomplete, more than twenty-one thousand colonists moved to New England in the 1630s, settling the coast from the Piscataqua River to Long Island Sound.

Under increasing pressure from ecclesiastical and civil authorities, John Cotton himself was removed from St. Botolph's Church and made the passage from Boston to Boston in 1633. The new Boston had a minister, but Cotton was recognized as pastor as well, appointed to the office of teacher. Every Thursday, he preached or lectured to large audiences in Boston. Cotton was the respected elder statesman of the New England church. Since the English episcopacy with its control and High Church liturgy did not follow the Puritan emigrants to the New World, the Puritan settlers were free to find their own way.

It was a new world indeed, where every citizen was equally part of the community, where the distinctions of rank and birth that formed English society were absent.

Just three years later, in 1636, Massachusetts Bay Company voted to allot four hundred pounds—half its annual tax receipts—for the founding of Harvard College. Where the college was located across the river became renamed Cambridge, and every effort was made to have the new college resemble as much as possible the colleges of Cambridge University—seat of Puritan intellectualism. Harvard College's *purpose* was to provide the new colony with a steady supply of educated Puritan ministers—free from all taint of Old World Anglicanism.

WEST IN THE CONNECTICUT RIVER VALLEY

In what is today Connecticut, settlement came first along the Connecticut River. Mightier and longer than any of England's waterways, the Connecticut was known then simply as "The Great River." Communities were established in the 1630s in Wethersfield, Windsor, and Hartford, as well as Saybrook, at the river's mouth, and farther west along the coast in New Haven.

Scouts exploring the river valley north of Hartford identified what is now Springfield, Massachusetts, as perfectly situated for settlement at a point where three tributaries entered the Connecticut. In 1636 William Pynchon led a settlement party upriver there to the first falls interrupting navigation, purchased land on both sides from the local natives, and named the new village Agawam Plantation.

Unlike Massachusetts Bay and Virginia, in a sense, along the Connecticut these were all independent colonies without a defined commission. The towns along the river united in 1637 to fight a local war with the Pequot Indians, but it was not until 1665 that King Charles II granted a royal charter to a unified Connecticut colony.

Following contention with the other Connecticut River settlements over dealings with the natives, in 1641 Pynchon's community voted to leave their confederation and annex themselves to Massachusetts Bay Colony. In due course, Pynchon was made magistrate of Agawam. The town was subsequently renamed Springfield after the East Anglian village where Pynchon grew up.

Ultimately, Springfield proved as well located as promised, the linchpin to settlements that grew north along the broad river in what is now known as the Pioneer Valley. For many years, however, Springfield was the westernmost town in Massachusetts Bay Colony.

ALL WAS NOT UNITY

While the Massachusetts Puritans might have been free to find their way, however, the same freedom did not extend to everyone, or for that matter, to *anyone* who did not share the accepted theological consensus of the community and its learned church leaders. Since his arrival in Boston in 1631, young Puritan divine Roger Williams had been something of a thorn in the side of that harmonious unity. With the ardent enthusiasm of the new convert, Williams believed the New England church was not sufficiently "Separated." At the same time, he taught that civil magistrates should not enforce church prohibitions such as Sabbath-breaking and blasphemy (a separation of church and state), and that individuals should be free to follow their own religious beliefs.

After several years of controversies with church leaders in several communities and the General Court, Williams was declared persona non grata in the colony. In 1636 Roger Williams and his small band of followers settled to the south of Plymouth territory on Narragansett Bay on land acquired from the Narragansett Indian sachems.

Williams named his settlement and proto-colony Providence. He purposed the community as a place where religious liberty was practiced and citizenship separated from church. The new de facto colony quickly became a safe zone attracting dissenters and dissidents already in the New World.

Roger Williams had been gravitating toward a belief in Believers Baptism, or credobaptism as the Anabaptists practiced the sacrament, for some time. In 1638 he was baptized—and organized what became the first Baptist Church in America. In the early 1640s Williams sailed to England and returned in 1644 with a charter from Parliament for Providence Plantation and Rhode Island (now Aquidneck Island).

THE ANTINOMIAN CONTROVERSY

The same eventful year that saw the founding of Harvard and settlement of Providence, 1636, saw as well the emergence of a religious and thus political controversy that would largely shape Massachusetts Bay and its neighboring colonies for seventy years. It became known as the Antinomian or Free Grace Controversy. The individual that prompted it was a strong-minded woman named Anne Hutchinson. Hutchinson had been a follower of John Cotton in England, and followed him to Boston.

The argument was whether divine grace was dependent wholly upon God's mercy, or whether your moral behaviors and perceivable godliness were the reliable evidence of God's grace and salvation.

As was not uncommon in English Puritan circles, she began holding conventicles—weekly meetings for women (and later men) to discuss the Sunday sermons—in her home. Hutchinson outspokenly criticized the colony's ministers for promoting a covenant of works, rather than a covenant of grace as taught by John Cotton. These people took this kind of thing seriously.

In brief, the argument was whether divine grace was dependent wholly upon God's mercy, or whether your moral behaviors and perceivable godliness were the reliable evidence of God's grace and salvation. Her exposition of Cotton's preaching on grace was accused of being "antinomian"—a belief that one's salvation, in fact, exempts one from the moral law. She became a popular and influential voice in what was then still a small town, as well as in its smaller suburbs.

The division of opinion upset the applecart of godly unity that was the shared vision of the Puritan colonists. When Anne Hutchinson finally was charged with sedition and brought before the General Court in November 1637, it became publicly obvious that she held several significant beliefs considered heterodox in Reformed theology. Most seriously, she claimed that the Holy Spirit spoke directly through her and provided new revelation. Reformed doctrine was unequivocal that the revelation of God came only from the Bible. Hutchinson didn't help her cause any when she charged the magistrates: "If you go on in this course you begin, you will bring a curse upon you and your posterity. And the mouth of the Lord hath spoken it."

Not surprisingly, the sentence of the court was banishment, "as being a woman not fit for our society." The following April, with her family and followers, Hutchinson accepted an invitation from Roger Williams in Providence and moved to Narragansett Bay. After her husband's death a few years later, Anne Hutchinson took her family and household to settle with the Dutch in New Netherland—in the Bronx near what became the Hutchinson River. The next August, 1643, Hutchinson and almost all her family were killed in an Indian attack.

SETTLING THE MASON GRANT

Anne Hutchinson was not the only casualty of the Antinomian controversy, however. Another major voice for the "covenant of grace" was Rev. John Wheelwright, who happened to be Hutchinson's brother-in-law. In a familiar story, Rev. Wheelwright was silenced in two English pulpits for his Puritan teachings. He arrived in Boston in 1636 to a warm welcome. Wheelwright is described as having a contentious disposition, however, and he quickly antagonized the "orthodox" majority from the pulpit and in his outspoken defense of Hutchinson. Wheelwright, too, was called before the General Court in November 1637. He, too, was banished from the colony for troubling the civil peace, having corrupt and dangerous opinions, and holding the magistrates in contempt.

The Bay Colony's border was the Merrimack River, which flows into the open Atlantic at Newburyport. Just a couple of years previously, Boston sent a small group of settlers north to build a village between the Parker and Merrimack Rivers, to solidify the Massachusetts Bay Colony's claim to its northern border.

The exiled Rev. John Wheelwright led his flock of 110 followers (some twenty families) above the Merrimack. In 1638, at the next

Newburyport: From Farm to Trade

Begun as the town of Newbury in 1635, Newburyport's story is typical of this 1630s settlement boom along the New England coast. The original township spread between the two rivers, which was relatively flat bottomland attractive for farming. What they found was an abundance of fish and a surfeit of lumber from clearing the land. These became the profitable cash crops, exported by sea. By the 1680s, at the mouth of the Merrimack, docks were built and shipbuilding began. A sea trade shipped timber and fish to the Caribbean in exchange for sugar and molasses—to be made into rum. Newburyport thrived with merchants, seamen, shipyards, and fishermen. In 1764 the bustling seaport separated from Newbury as Newburyport and continued to prosper. Newbury remained a smaller community of farmers.

Newburyport's Custom House Maritime Museum superbly tells the story of the town's glory years as a center of shipbuilding and sea trade. Pride of place belongs to the gallery devoted to the United States Coast Guard—born here in 1791 with the commissioning of the cutter *Massachusetts*.

principal estuary to the north, the Piscataqua River, the band turned in along the shores of Great Bay and settled New Hampshire's first town, Exeter. There, they ordered a Congregational Church.

Later, Wheelwright pastored in Hampton before returning to Lincolnshire in 1655 during the Commonwealth. A personal friend and college mate of Oliver Cromwell's, Wheelwright took the church in Alford until the Restoration. When the tables turned and things became hot for Puritans in the early 1660s, Wheelwright returned to New England and served as minister in Salisbury, Massachusetts, for seventeen years until his death at eighty-seven in 1679.

While it was the teaching of John Cotton that ultimately caused the furor in the fledgling colony, Cotton's fate was very different. From the beginning, he obviously had a store of social capital and a gravitas in the colony that both Hutchinson and Wheelwright lacked. Beyond that, however, Cotton's demeanor and wisdom in handling those with whom he disagreed contrasted markedly with Wheelwright's confrontations and Hutchinson's imprecations (after all, he had plenty of experience). Though Cotton offered to leave the community, he was urged to remain, and continued as a minister in Boston until his death in 1652. Cotton's 1642 book *The Way of Congregational Churches Cleared* became the blueprint for what became known as the Congregational Way, or the New England Way.

The Antinomian Controversy had a defining impact on Massachusetts Bay that would characterize the society for decades. The primary requirement for membership in the community was conformity—both religious and social. The banishment of Hutchinson and Wheelwright was not simply an insistence on theological purity, but to eliminate the dissension itself. Their worldview was that a divided community could not effectively be that "city on a hill" that was their motivating ideal. The crime of Anne Hutchinson was only incidentally or proximately over the doctrinal difference per se, but the very *difference* itself and its impact or potential impact upon civil unity.

In both the church meeting and the town meeting, every decision was sought by consensus. The drawback was a society that could certainly feel repressive—and result in such harsh and shameful consequences as

The Paradigm of Exeter

When Rev. John Wheelwright and his church community were effectively banished from Massachusetts Bay in 1638 little did they know that their exodus would become something of a prototype for the settlement pattern of the four New England colonies—New Hampshire, Massachusetts, Rhode Island, and Connecticut—for the next century.

Wheelwright's group sent a scouting party ahead to find a suitable place to settle and rebuild their homes, church, and lives. Sailing up the Piscatagua River from Portsmouth Harbor and into the massive Great Bay estuary, they followed a broad tributary river, navigable for several miles before reaching a rock ladder of falls. Above the falls, the river is fresh, flowing from the west (now named the Exeter River); below the falls, the Squamscot River is tidal and brackish.

From unknown time, the location had proven a rich fishing grounds for the native Penacook Indians. The Wheelwright party purchased large swathes of the Squamscot River valley and western shoreline of Great Bay from Wehanownowit, a Penacook sagamore. Here at the falls they made the destination of their exodus. It was a perfect location.

New England is virtually entirely encompassed as a part of North America's Great North Woods, glacier-scrubbed and thickly forested. Natural meadows or grasslands are almost nonexistent; wetlands are many; topsoil is often thin and invariably rock filled. Along the river valleys, however, ground was flatter, topsoil thicker, and the land relatively easy to clear for farming. And Exeter's Squamscot River, navigable to the sea, provided for the easy movement of people, goods, and commerce to Portsmouth's harbor (then Strawbery Banke), Boston, and England.

Most important of all, however, were the falls themselves. The one amenity that any farming community of the seventeenth century certainly needed was a mill or two. A gristmill ground grain of any variety into flour and cattle feed. A sawmill cut the trees felled with the clearing of the land into timbers and planks for the building of homes, barns, and boats—and for export. The Exeter River falls provided the power for both. The next year, Exeter had its gristmill, built by Thomas Wilson on an island in the lower falls. The sawmill followed a few years later.

One of the original four townships of New Hampshire, Exeter can lay some claim to being the first proper *town*. That is, the community was organized at their settlement to make their first business the ordering of their church. The large white clapboard Congregational church with the steeple in the center of Exeter today proclaims on its signboard its role as the oldest church in the state.

Where the mill and the church were located, the town grew up along the riverfront. Docks were built to land the shallow-draft gundalows that ferried colonists, timber, salt fish, and English goods; Water Street took shape along the waterfront with residences and soon enough merchants and a tavern. The town prospered.

Here the Exeter River splits over falls and becomes the tidal Squamscot River flowing into Great Bay. The low mustard-colored buildings on an island in the middle of the falls stand on the site of Exeter's first gristmill, built in 1640.

Subsequently, while Portsmouth was the colonial capital for much of the next century and a half, Exeter weighed heavily in colonial affairs and grew in affluence. During the years of struggle for independence from Britain in the 1770s, Exeter served as capital, a town full of active Sons of Liberty, and here signed the colony's own Declaration of Independence six months before the Declaration at the Continental Congress in Philadelphia. When that document was adopted, copies were immediately dispatched to each of the colonial capitals. When New Hampshire's copy arrived in Exeter on July 14, 1776, it was read aloud in the town center. The document resides in town today at the American Independence Museum in the home of the state treasurer at the time, John Gilman, and is read every year during the town's independence celebration on that date.

The factors of its settlement are still very visible in Exeter today. Standing on the walkway along the Squamscot River, you can see its tidal nature below the falls, and the island in the middle with low, old mustard-colored buildings where the original mill once stood. On the western side, the riverfront backs of commercial buildings line Water Street, the town's bustling downtown, just as they did in the 1640s. These same factors defined the establishment of settlements, villages, and towns along the coast as immigration from England continued through the 1600s. There were no roads. Travel beyond the coast was by water, and went no farther than the fall lines of the navigable rivers allowed. There, the falls allowed good fishing and power for mills. It would be well into the 1700s before rudimentary roads dug out of often rugged and thickly forested country brought developing inland communities.

Puritan Practicality:
New England Baked Beans

One of the most ubiquitous and well-known of New England regional comestibles is the humble baked bean, which dates from the earliest Puritan years. Saturday was baking day, and most kitchen fireplaces, however humble, had a bread oven to the side of the fire. A pot of beans tucked in the back of the oven would bake through the afternoon with the bread and pie for supper that night. The residual heat of the oven would then keep the leftover beans warm overnight, and they would make a substantive Sunday breakfast before the trip to the meeting house for the long morning church service.

Here's an old farm-family recipe that goes back at least to the mid 1800s. Take one pound of dry beans—pea beans, navy beans, or kidney beans—rinse and soak overnight in plenty of water. The next day, bring to a parboil for up to half an hour before using. The test is to blow onto several beans in a spoon. If the skin curls back, they are ready to bake (in a ceramic bean pot, of course).

2 tbsp. of brown sugar

2–3 tbsp. of dark molasses

1 rounded tsp. of dry mustard

12 oz. piece of salt pork cut in several pieces or several slices of bacon cut in pieces, or alternatively 1 tbsp. of bacon fat

1 tbsp. of salt (less if using salt pork)

1 medium onion, cut roughly in eighths

(Optional: add half a tsp. of dry ginger or 1 tsp. dry thyme)

Make a slurry of the seasonings in the bean pot with water from the beans. Ladle beans into pot with pork and onion pieces in layers reserving the last for the top. Add bean water to cover. Bake uncovered at 325 for roughly two hours. Check periodically and add bean liquor to cover as necessary. Then, in or out of the stove, putting the bean pot cover on will keep them hot for a long time.

the Salem Witch Trials of the 1690s. The advantage was that in a hard, dangerous, and wild new land, small communities could thrive because of their unity of purpose.

The advantage was that in a hard, dangerous, and wild new land, small communities could thrive because of their unity of purpose.

In 1653 Strawbery Banke became Portsmouth, named for the county of Hampshire's port city, home of the Royal Navy. As it happens, Portsmouth, *New* Hampshire, has been for generations the northernmost Atlantic coast American naval base. As for John Mason, though he spent years in North America, he died in 1635 while planning his first voyage to his new colony. For the next hundred years, New Hampshire was the northwestern frontier between the English colonies and both the French and the native Indians.

CHAPTER 8

Between the Colonies:
An Active and Uncertain Age

There's a reason the Exodus story has inspired so many Americans. It is a narrative of hope.

—BRUCE FEILOR

BETWEEN THE RELIGIOUSLY MOTIVATED EXODUS OF PURITANS TO NEW England and the economic adventurers seeking their fortune in the Virginia Tidewater there was a lot of Atlantic coastline. This was still all virtually fair game for settlement and colonization in the early 1600s. As Francois Rabelais has often been quoted as saying, "Nature abhors a vacuum," and so does available, unclaimed land. After a century of religious conflict throughout Europe, there were plenty of peoples who were ready to seek a New World.

A CATHOLIC REFUGE IN MARYLAND
The Puritans were not the only ones being hounded by King Charles's Anglican establishment. Under King James there had been a reasonable tolerance, but his son Charles outlawed Roman Catholicism. An English colony in America might provide a refuge for them as well.

In the first decades of the seventeenth century, there were many among the English educated class who had a strong interest in the New World and the constant flow of the new discoveries being reported back across the Atlantic. It was a topic of discussion, and young boys grew up dreaming of crossing the ocean on adventures just as a twenty-first-century teen might aspire to become an astronaut. Among them was an ambitious, determined lad from North Yorkshire who had grown up with Catholic gentry parents, constantly in trouble for their nonconformity.

George Calvert was born at his knighted father's manor, Kiplin Hall, in Richmondshire, an area notorious in its time for its adherence to the Catholic faith. Calvert escaped the turmoil and the north in 1594 to Trinity College, Oxford. At the time, he would certainly have had to subscribe to the oath of allegiance, pledging his conformity to the Church of England. Calvert obviously knew the way to success. After taking a degree in foreign languages, Calvert followed that route to London and studied law for several years at Lincoln's Inn.

A meeting with Sir Robert Cecil on the Continent in 1603 brought Calvert into the service of one of the chief architects of King James I's succession that year. That was the break that Calvert needed. With his facility in the European languages, as well as Latin, and his legal education, Calvert was well equipped to take advantage, rising through the ranks of King James's court and retinue as an ambassador, trouble-shooter, and privy counselor to become one of two principal secretaries of state in 1619.

His years of political success and connections made Calvert wealthy, but not invulnerable. In 1621 Calvert became the principal Parliamentary spokesman for an unpopular marriage alliance proposed between the king's son, Charles, the Prince of Wales, and a princess of Catholic Spain. When the proposal fell apart, George Calvert's political influence crashed. The aging King James rewarded his loyalty in 1623 with a twenty-three-hundred-acre estate in County Longford, Ireland, and raised him to the Irish peerage as Baron Baltimore. Calvert was savvy enough to know that his power had passed, however, and resigned office in 1625. Shortly thereafter, Calvert made public his conversion to Catholicism.

Throughout his career, Calvert had maintained a serious interest in the discovery-in-progress going on along the eastern Atlantic seaboard. In 1609 he had taken a small stake in the Virginia Company, and later he invested in the fledgling East India Company. In 1620 Calvert purchased a peninsula of the island of Newfoundland and called his holding Avalon. The next year, he commissioned a captain and a shipload of Welsh colonists to construct a settlement at a fishing station named Ferryland. It became the first permanent English settlement in Canada.

Calvert saw Avalon as an economic venture, holding promise for fisheries, furs, timber, and agriculture. Early reports from the colony were optimistic and seemed to corroborate Calvert's plans. More settlers landed and the fledgling colony appeared to be doing well. After Calvert left office in 1625, he planned an expedition to his New World palatinate. He finally sailed to Avalon in 1627 and stayed two months. The mild Atlantic summer was deceptive, but Calvert was convinced the future lay there. The next year he returned with his family and another shipload of settlers to take charge of his proprietary colony. That next winter of 1628/29 did in Calvert and the colony, hitting Newfoundland with severe cold and Atlantic storms that continued into May. Calvert returned to England that summer in disgust, convinced his efforts had been futilely placed and that the only hope of success lay in a colony farther south.

Now Lord Baltimore, Calvert determined to establish a colony deliberately designed as a New World haven for English Catholics.

By this time, now Lord Baltimore, Calvert determined to establish a colony deliberately designed as a New World haven for English Catholics. King James had been succeeded several years previously by the young King Charles. Calvert had lost much of his influence in the new court, but after much negotiation, and despite the objections of Virginia colonists, in 1632 Baltimore received a grant on the north Chesapeake and what leter came to be called the Delmarva Peninsula. Alas, the 1st Baron Baltimore died just a few weeks before the royal seal was affixed to the colonial paperwork.

Though George Calvert is often credited with the establishment of the colony of Maryland, in fact, the grant passed to his oldest son, Cecil Calvert, who became the 2nd Baron Baltimore. It is this Lord Baltimore for whom the modern city is named.

In March 1634 the first settlers of the new colony, led by Leonard Calvert, Cecil's younger brother, landed much farther south on a peninsula on the west side of Chesapeake Bay. The community was St. Mary's City; Leonard served as the first governor of the proprietary colony. From the beginning, Roman Catholics were recruited to come to Maryland, named putatively for the queen, Henrietta Marie, but possibly as well for St. Mary the Virgin. It was the first colony that practiced full religious tolerance.

Catholics were indeed free, and from the beginning many Catholics played leadership roles as the colony grew. Roman Catholics were never a majority community in the colony, however, though it became the principal port of Catholic entry into colonial America for generations.

New Netherlands in the Mid-Atlantic

The French were adventuring along the northern coastland of what became the Canadian Maritimes, and certainly the St. Lawrence beckoned them inland. But they were not the only other European power to be exploring the New World in the early 1600s.

An English ship's captain who had been at sea since he was a cabin boy, Henry Hudson, was hired in 1609 by the Dutch East India Company to find a fabled northeast passage that would lead over the Arctic Circle to Asia and the exotic market ports of Cathay. Aboard the Dutch ship *Halve Maen* (Half Moon), Hudson sailed the coast from Newfoundland to Cape Cod and as far south as Chesapeake Bay, then explored the principal river estuaries he encountered on his way back up the coast. He put in to the estuary of the river that now bears his name and in September 1609 sailed ten days upriver to Albany. When Hudson returned to the Netherlands with his report and a ship's cargo of furs late that year, his accounts established Dutch claims to the Hudson River Valley and the islands in its estuary.

Of course, Hudson had failed in his commission, not coming close to locating the elusive Northwest Passage. In 1610, with English backers this time, Hudson set out again, on a more northerly route across the Atlantic. This trip, in the ship *Discovery*, Hudson found the Hudson Strait leading above Labrador into ocean-sized Hudson Bay. Hudson spent the months exploring its shores in search of the Passage, then wintered over with his crew onshore. The next spring Hudson intended to carry on the voyage to the west. In brief, his crew outvoted him with a mutiny. Hudson and a small loyal party were set adrift with supplies in a small boat and never heard from again.

At the mouth of the Hudson River, the Dutch formally proclaimed the province of New Netherland in 1614—including Long Island, Manhattan, northern New Jersey, and the navigable Hudson River as far north as their trading post at Fort Orange, present-day Albany. For a decade, the region largely remained in the hands of fur traders, principally seeking beaver pelts and often bartering with local Indians.

In 1625 Dutch settlers arrived and laid out Fort Amsterdam, soon called New Amsterdam, on the southern tip of Manhattan. It was a perfect location to control access to the Hudson. The village was made capital of the province with Peter Minuit appointed director-general of the colony in 1626. Minuit famously negotiated the purchase of Manhattan Island from the Lenape Indians for a peppercorn price.

The Dutch certainly had the maritime expertise to support their new colony. Over the next generation they spread small communities around the Hudson estuary and north into the river valley. In fact, however, the Dutch venture was largely commercial—an economic opportunity. The political and religious incentives to immigration that propelled the slow but steady growth of New England and Virginia through the mid-1600s weren't factors in the Calvinist, Reformed Netherlands.

Today we think of both Amsterdam and Manhattan as world-class urban centers. In actuality, despite being the provincial capital, New Amsterdam numbered a population of a scant three hundred by the 1650s. The Dutch province was left alone during the English Commonwealth of that decade. After all, the Reformed Dutch were coreligionists with the controlling Puritans. With the Restoration of the monarchy and Anglican ecclesiology, however, it was only a matter of time before England would see the vulnerable Dutch foothold to be an obstacle to its hegemony along the Atlantic coast from Maine to Georgia.

In August 1664 four English men-of-war sailed into the Hudson estuary and effectively took control of New Amsterdam. The following

June, the town was reorganized under English jurisdiction and renamed New York, after King Charles II's brother James, Duke of York. The Dutch retaliated with several naval skirmishes, but finally settled the matter by treaty. To this day, Dutch place-names abound in metropolitan New York and spreading north along the Hudson River Valley. And who can forget Rip Van Winkle?

TROUBLES ROCK THE ENGLISH PEACE

The constant harassment caused by the Laws of Conformity was a contributing factor to the flood of Puritan immigration to growing New England. As far as King Charles was concerned, though, he was glad to be rid of them and their influence. Finally, however, the rigid monarch took a step too far. It foolishly became King Charles's aim to foist English Episcopal practice on his native land. The Scots would have none of it.

The Protestant nobles and clergy of Scotland were emphatic: No bishops. James's attempts at coercing the Kirks' compliance unleashed a torrent of bad feeling. The National Covenant of 1581 had pledged to keep the Scottish Kirk Presbyterian and Reformed. The revived National Covenant was ceremonially signed in Greyfriars Churchyard in February 1638, and copies were dispatched around the country for signing. Its signatories became known as Covenanters, and the Covenanters were prepared to use force and expend their lives in keeping their word. In 1640 the Scottish Parliament adopted the Covenant—to which all citizens were expected to subscribe.

With religious fervor running high, the Covenanters called forth an army to resist King Charles and his religious impositions. They succeeded in driving Charles out of Scotland and its Kirk, but by now the king had bigger problems of his own making.

The historic role of Parliament was being challenged by an absolutist monarch squarely in the face of a revolution in the marketplace of ideas.

Through the 1630s the divergent political agendas of King Charles and his Parliament were hardening. London, East Anglia, and the Midlands were strongly Puritan and fervent supporters of Parliament. The West Country and the North were areas of strong support for the king. In the eyes of King Charles and his Royalist supporters, the king's authority was absolute and the responsibility of his loyal subjects was to support the king's "prerogatives." In the eyes of a Parliament with a two-hundred-year growing tradition of being consulted and having advise-and-consent power in matters of taxation, the king was attempting to change the traditions and role of the English monarchy—violating principles dating back to 1215's Magna Carta.

To that stark political conflict of principles, the divide between the parties was fueled by passionately felt religious convictions, particularly on the part of the Parliament-backing Puritans. The historic role of Parliament was being challenged by an absolutist monarch squarely in the face of a revolution in the marketplace of ideas that fanned the aspirations and self-confidence of those not born into the bloodlines of the all-powerful, titled nobility backing the king.

New England's Slow March to Democracy

It's a long-held truism, up in New England at least, that the old-fashioned New England town meeting is America's purest form of democracy. To the extent that town meeting, the AGM of the incorporated township, continues to be the meaningful vehicle of local government, this still may be as true now as it was three hundred years ago.

We generally associate early New England with the American democratic impulse for several reasons: the Mayflower Compact and William Bradford's *On Plymouth Plantation*, the early firebrands of the movement for American independence, for instance, as well as the famous town meeting form of local government.

Democracy and its values of citizenship and social equality were quite the natural by-product of the Reformed Protestant ethos that the Puritans brought with them from England. The institutionalization and application of that new Protestant concept of the natural equality of individuals, however, took several generations to evolve in New England society.

Both the relationship of the individual to society (the local community) and the relationship between the local town and the central colonial government were very different here in the New World from what they were in England. With every generation that passed, New England colonists had fewer ties with, less knowledge of, and less loyalty to the social mores and political cultural of the mother country.

The settlement of Massachusetts Bay in 1630, with the avowed intention of setting up a godly society, was governed by Biblical principles as taught from the pulpit by Puritan preachers. Their "city on a hill" may not have been a theocracy, but it was theocratic in spirit. As settlements radiated from Boston and along the coast from Cape Cod to Cape Elizabeth, the minister of the local church was the most important leader in the community. His moral authority, however, stemmed from his call as minister by the church—once again, a call that was not by majority vote, but generally by consensus.

As settlement in Massachusetts spread along the coast and inland via the river valleys through the 1600s, the colonial government back in Boston became further removed from the settlement communities and the lives of its colonists. Their local communities, villages, and townships were everything. Their ability to survive and thrive on the frontier in the New England climate vitally depended upon their solidarity as a community, and very little on the doings of a remote central government—be it Boston or London. Consensus, then, was the guiding principle of local decision making not just in calling the town's minister, but in every significant community decision.

To say the least, the villages that spread through Massachusetts, Rhode Island, Connecticut, and New Hampshire were homogenous communities. These were all English settlers who shared a past, a culture, a worldview, and a religion. They were also *small* communities, numbering their population in the dozens, not the thousands. Finding consensus on building a new road between the village and nearest market town is actually possible in a community of 120 people.

If each individual's consent was desired in community decisions, then each individual's voice was significant. In the early years, meetings of the community to make decisions were held in the meeting house, appropriately enough. That was the church.

Inevitably, Massachusetts Bay Colony grew and expanded farther and farther from Boston. So, too, did the emerging colonization of Connecticut along Long Island Sound—Old Lyme, Mystic, Saybrook, Groton, New London, and New Haven. And in New Hampshire from the Merrimack to Portsmouth and around Great Bay. Such homogeneity of belief demanded by the upshot of the Antinomian Controversy back in 1638 became impossible to maintain.

The impulse of villages and townships to govern themselves by sustaining a local commonality of belief and practice, a practical consensus in religious as well as civic affairs, survived well into the eighteenth century. Inevitably, however, the New England colonies and their constituent communities became increasingly diverse.

New England's first concession to the separation of church and state came when they separated the town meeting and business space from the community church. Often that was accomplished in the same building. The town hall filled the lower floor, while the church was upstairs. Many such town buildings still stand on the green in villages across New England today, often still serving one (and in rare instances both) of their original functions.

Even when the colonial government advanced enough to pass voting requirements upon its citizens, generally those were ignored in the localities and every male was entitled to a vote in local elections. Voters elected selectmen to serve as executives, seeing that the decisions of the community were effected. They also elected minor officers to do such things as round up stray animals and monitor the boundaries of town and personal properties.

Townships also elected representatives to the colonial assembly. While today we assume that our congressmen and senators are virtual representatives, in colonial times delegates to such assemblies were sent explicitly to voice and vote the directives of the local community. A representative who showed any independence from their commission was disgraced and soon replaced.

BULLETIN: THE OUTBREAK OF WAR

After a prolonged period of rising tensions, in 1642 King Charles made an ill-advised attempt to arrest four leaders of his recalcitrant House of Commons. Being warned of the midnight plot, the Puritan MPs escaped. A raid on Parliament by the king's men at night, however, was an outrage that enflamed the city of London. It became a city at arms.

Events of the next decade would have reverberations through the formation, definition, and history of the fledgling English colonies across the Atlantic.

The king and his court rightly found the atmosphere in London too hostile for their safety. King Charles and his retinue decamped to loyal Oxford, where the king raised his standard and called his loyal peerage to arms. Though few people on either side could have imagined such at the time, the stage was set for what became known as the English Civil War. And no one could have imagined how those events of the next decade would have reverberations through the formation, definition, and history of the fledgling English colonies across the Atlantic.

CHAPTER 9

England in Civil War

What is all our histories, but God showing himself, shaking and tram-
pling on everything that he has not planted.
—OLIVER CROMWELL

THE NATURAL SENTIMENTS OF THE NEW ENGLAND COLONIALS, OF
course, were with the Puritan cause in Parliament. Virginians, certainly
anyone who had a voice, felt loyalties of kinship and religion with the
Royalist Party. In the 1640s, these were still the only significant English
outposts in North America. Inevitably, the progress and the outcome of
the war had a huge impact on the fledgling Atlantic colonies.

THE KING AND PARLIAMENT RISE TO ARMS

The first full-scale conflict of the Civil War was the Battle of Edgehill,
fought near the Cotswolds in November 1642. The Royalist army was
victorious, but not by much. The tactical outcome was largely a draw. In
succeeding smaller battles and skirmishes the early Royalist success continued. In 1644 Parliament reorganized its army under the command of
Thomas Fairfax and Oliver Cromwell: It became the New Model Army.
Fairfax organized the infantry, while Cromwell—the only MP allowed a
commission in the New Model Army—commanded the cavalry.

In retrospect, the ultimate outcome of the war militarily was fore-
ordained from that point. The Royalist armies of King Charles were
raised and led in the same way that they had been for centuries. The king
raised his standard and called his nobles to assemble with their knights,

retainers, and armed vassals. From the time of the Norman Conquest, these feudal tenants-in-chief held their lands and titles from the king, in part in return for their armed service as necessary. The peers' own tenants and retainers in turn held their land and livings under the same terms. When the lord called out his tenants, they became troops for the duration of the campaign.

Regardless of their military experience, prowess, or leadership skills, the nobles and knights commanded those private armies they brought to the field. In this case, though the quality of Royalist commanders on the field varied, King Charles was fortunate to have in Prince Rupert a field general experienced in the European wars, who also happened to be his nephew. Royalists scored significant victories in the war's first year.

Parliament, however, called for an army of freemen, laborers, townsmen, and gentry, who would be paid for their service. Their officers were to be chosen and promoted not on the basis of social rank but on their military prowess and fitness for leadership. That is, their leaders were chosen on merit and ability. In that sense, the New Model Army was the world's first professional military organization. Fairfax and Cromwell proved successful and charismatic leaders, and Oliver Cromwell came to be among the most effective cavalry commanders in European history. The tide of the war militarily inevitably turned to favor Parliament.

At the Battle of Marston Moor in 1643 and the Battle of Naseby in 1644, the Puritan army of Parliament, much more highly motivated and better led, inflicted serious and bloody defeats on the Royalist army—and effectively ended the king's chances at a military victory. In both of these battles, Cromwell's disciplined cavalry played a decisive role in the victory of Parliament's New Model Army.

CREATING A ROYALIST REFUGE IN VIRGINIA

Meanwhile, the king had made a royal appointment that was to prove a lifeline for Royalists long after the Civil War. In August 1641 an ambitious young privy councilor won appointment as the royal governor of Virginia. From a cadet branch of the historic and titled Berkeley family, Sir William Berkeley brought both connections and ability to the role— along with a determination to make his mark in Virginia.

Like his older brothers, William Berkeley had received a gentleman's education and followed them to Oxford. With a bright wit and due networking, Berkeley received a place in King Charles's court and joined the unending queue for preferment and opportunity. His role as a privy councilor was largely that of a glorified errand boy with a few minor administrative duties. He accompanied Charles north in the Second Bishop's War and acquitted himself well enough to receive a knighthood.

Berkeley campaigned shrewdly for the post in Virginia, and, in truth, King Charles was paying little attention to his distant colony. He was busy contending with Parliament and getting ready to fight yet again the recalcitrant Scots Presbyterians. There were still only around eight thousand colonists in Virginia when Sir William Berkeley was appointed governor of the colony. Along with his connections, Sir William brought to Virginia energy, vision, a sense of purpose, and utter loyalty to the Crown.

He arrived in Jamestown and was inaugurated with little ceremony on March 8, 1642, only five months before full-scale war broke out at Edgehill that November.

Early on, Berkeley showed deftness for Virginia's colonial politics. He created a bicameral legislature with an appointed council and an elected general assembly of burgesses. Berkeley's very success threatened the indigenous Indians. The aging chieftain Opechancanough judged that with a new governor, the colonists might be vulnerable. Massing his forces undetected, Opechancanough launched a coordinated attack on April 18, 1644, on Maundy Thursday.

More than five hundred colonists were killed in the surprise onslaughts. Others died or were taken captive as fighting spread over the next few days. A hastily summoned meeting of the general assembly resulted in Berkeley being commissioned to return to England to seek military hardware and royal assistance. He sailed in June, but arrived to find the king and his cause in disarray, the war going badly and no help available. Rather than take a commission with his brothers in the king's army, Berkeley bought up what weapons he could procure and made back for Virginia. He landed in Jamestown in June 1645—a year after setting out.

The Indian war with Opechancanough was not going well either. On his return, Berkeley took personal charge of the militia and the conduct of the war. By the following spring, the militia had run Opechancanough to ground, captured him, and brought him to Jamestown. The plan was to ship him to England, but a militiaman bayoneted the Indian leader while he lay in the town jail. The war, however, was over.

Berkeley drafted a first-ever Anglo-Indian treaty, ratified by the general assembly in October 1646. Among the provisions, the Indians agreed to be governed by English colonial law rather than tribal custom. In return, the Indians received protected lands north of the York River. While the treaty guided relations between the English and Indians for several decades, the tide of English settlers overwhelmed even William Berkeley's best honorable intentions. The Indians were inevitably pushed farther and farther west and south.

A landed family might hedge their bets in the uncertain Civil War, sending a younger son to Virginia with the wherewithal to begin a plantation.

With the conflict flaring in England, Governor Berkeley's vision was simple. He purposed to make Virginia friendly to investment and settlement for royalist gentlemen. While the estates and primary title of a noble family might be settled on an eldest son in the custom of primogeniture, a landed family might hedge their bets in the uncertain Civil War, sending a younger son to Virginia with the wherewithal to begin a plantation. The result would protect a portion of the family's assets against the fortunes of war, and create a revenue stream not dependent upon the uncertain climate in England.

Berkeley's was a timely and successful strategy. As the war increasingly went against the interests of the king and his party in the mid 1640s, more and more families took advantage of Berkeley's enticement. Unlike the Puritan colonists to New England, these nascent Virginians brought with them the resources to begin plantations—money enough for large tracts of land and substantial country houses, with indentured servants to do the backbreaking labor.

Thousands of new colonists arrived in Virginia through the 1640s. Their pattern of settlement followed that of New England, as they spread plantations and small communities along the navigable tidewater rivers that fed Chesapeake Bay, the tributaries of the James and York Rivers, and then northward to the Rappahannock. Berkeley put his energies into building Jamestown as the colonial capital, attracting artisans and merchants. For the first time, the colony began to feel successful and stable. In a few short decades it would become the most prosperous and populous of the English American colonies.

The society these planters built under Governor Berkeley's leadership bore little resemblance to the communities of freeholding Congregationalists that emerged in New England. In Virginia, loyalty to the Crown meant loyalty to the established Church of England. It also meant a hierarchical society governed by the same conventions of common law and social institutions that had defined English society since William the Conqueror.

As the balance of power swung from the intractable Stuart monarch to the military force of Parliament, the tide of emigration from England to the New World swung from New England to Virginia. In fact, through the 1640s and 1650s there was little net migration into New England. After all, the Puritan cause was their cause. Numbers of families and young men actually returned from Massachusetts Bay to England to aid in the struggle.

ENDGAME FOR THE WAR AND EXECUTION OF A KING

King Charles had been taken in 1646 and surrendered to the Scots Covenanters. There followed something of a brokered peace with Parliament. The king was in essence paroled on good behavior. When Charles and his followers renewed the conflict, however, Parliament became increasingly radical and determined upon his abdication at the least.

When King Charles attempted to entice Scotland to join him at arms and invade England in his support, Parliament charged the king with treason against his own people. The rather bumbling monarch's fate was sealed. Parliamentary forces took the king's person a second time in 1648, and he was held captive in the secure fortress of Carisbrooke Castle on the Isle of Wight. When Parliament was ready for him, King Charles was conveyed (with enormous respect for his person) first to Windsor, and then to Westminster for trial.

There was little doubt concerning the outcome, but then there was little doubt that the unhappy Stuart king was guilty as charged.

Virtually the entire sitting Parliament still remaining since the beginning of war disrupted the normal administration of government sat as a jury to hear the charges against the king—some forty elected members of the Commons. There was little doubt concerning the outcome, but then, there was little doubt that the unhappy Stuart king was guilty as charged. What was without precedent, however, was the excruciatingly difficult decision to execute the king. Even for a Parliament collectively tired of war, impatient with King Charles's repeated perfidy, and convinced of the righteousness of their action, signing the warrant for the beheading of a sitting king would have been an agonizingly difficult choice.

Nonetheless, it was done. The execution of King Charles was the first judicial execution of a king in known history. After all, the king was God's anointed. He may not have been entitled to the absolute authority he demanded, but he was to many an earthly vicar in the hierarchy of God's intentions—and to kill him?

On January 31, 1649, King Charles I stepped from a window of the banqueting hall of Whitehall Palace onto a constructed scaffold, where he was ceremoniously beheaded in front of an emotional throng filling Whitehall. Charles took his fate with utmost dignity, wearing two shirts to prevent him from shivering lest the assembled onlookers think that he showed fear.

When the sword came down and the king's head left his shoulders, it is said that an audible and instinctive collective groan emerged from the crowd. No matter what their politics, religious convictions, or engagement in the late Civil War might have been, the execution of the king disturbed the collective unconscious of many people and the known, shared history of all.

THE ACCIDENTAL COMMONWEALTH

What now? There had never not been a king. The complete control of government, and the fate of England, lay in the rump Parliament. To their responsibility fell the organization of a new form of government. It became known as the Commonwealth. Resolving the matter of who would be head of state, let alone head of government, was only one of myriad details to be dealt with by Parliament in the immediate aftermath of the king's beheading.

The Royal Stuart family remaining fled to France, home country of Queen Henrietta Marie, and the protection of the reigning Catholic family. Though the military outcome had long been determined, King Charles I's execution was the effective end of the Civil War. The New Model Army that was ensconced in and around London during the king's trial and execution had done their job, and Puritan England rejoiced.

Parliament then sent Cromwell and the army to Ireland in August 1649 to pacify the Catholic Irish who had risen to champion the son of Charles I. The uncrowned King Charles II returned to Britain to rally Royalists, including many Scots, for one last clash with Cromwell's army. At the Battle of Worcester in September, 1651, the New Model Army crushed the Royalist army and hopes—with three thousand dead and roughly ten thousand taken prisoner. A majority of those were duly deported to the New World as indentured servants. Charles II escaped by the skin of his teeth and made his way back to the Continent.

Now the Civil War was over. With the war won, however, there was no foreseeable need of a standing army. Parliament was ready to disperse the regiments and dismiss the soldiers to return home and resume their lives.

This was the professional New Model Army, however, one that was recruited, trained, and fought for pay rather than as part of a feudal obligation. Now, it was also time to pay the army, and Parliament had no funds with which to do so. This was an immediate fly in the proverbial

"Warts and All":
Who Was This Oliver Cromwell?

"I would have been glad to have lived under my wood side, and to have kept a flock of sheep, rather than to have undertaken this government."
—OLIVER CROMWELL

The difference between a life of obscurity and a historic role on the world's stage is often a matter of being in the right (or wrong) place at the right time. A country squire rising through the ranks of the army and being named head of state and head of government is hardly a planned fate.

Oliver Cromwell was born in April 1599 in Huntingdon, a market town some twenty miles northwest of Cambridge, into a family of minor gentry—country gentlemen, but hardly aristocracy. Oliver was given a sound education at Huntingdon's local grammar school.

At the time, East Anglia was a hotbed of Puritan ideology and conviction, particularly among the literate middling class to which the Cromwells belonged. At home and at school, Cromwell would have absorbed the radical Reformation notion of the personal responsibility of individuals before God. In 1616 he entered Sidney Sussex College at Cambridge.

The death of Cromwell's father interrupted his university tenure and he returned to manage the family lands and care for his mother. In 1620 he studied law at London's Inns of Court, and married Elizabeth Bourchier with whom he would have nine children. They returned to settle near the family's holdings in Ely. What became the family home stands today just two hundred yards across the green from majestic Ely Cathedral. The country squire was elected to Parliament in 1628 and again, representing Cambridge, in 1640.

Oliver Cromwell was a man of Puritan conviction and voice, but not an important leader in Parliament, a middle-aged country squire with five children and no military experience. When hostilities between king and Parliament broke out in 1642, Cromwell returned to Ely and recruited a troop of horsemen, which he captained and led into the Battle of Edgehill that October.

In February 1643 Cromwell was appointed colonel in the army of the Eastern Association of seven counties formed to defend and advance Parliament's cause in East Anglia. He quickly raised a regiment. By August Cromwell had become Lieutenant General of the Horse—commander of the cavalry. The keys to his success were his insistence on good treatment of his soldiers and strict discipline from them.

Hardly the stately residence we expect of a national leader, Oliver Cromwell's modest house in Ely is now a visitor attraction and the small cathedral city's Tourist Information Centre.

Cromwell's then unheard-of insistence upon appointing officers based upon their character and ability rather than the gentility of their background caused clashes with his titled and experienced military superiors. Yet Cromwell continued to win battles over the Royalists, at Gainsborough, Winceby, and Lincoln.

The Association army joined the main Parliamentary army of Lord Fairfax and regiments of Scottish Covenanters in York. There it clashed with the largest Royalist force in the field, commanded by King Charles's nephew, Prince Rupert of the Rhine. At the Battle of Marston Moor (July 2, 1644), involving more than forty-two thousand combatants, the armies of Parliament routed the Royalists decisively, thanks principally to Cromwell's command of five thousand cavalry troops. The combined army of Scots and Parliamentarians lost three hundred men. The Royalists left four thousand dead and fifteen hundred captured. Cromwell's reputation as a leader and a cavalry commander was secured.

That autumn Parliament reorganized what became the New Model Army. In many respects, this became the first professional army in the world. Members of the House of Lords or Commons were excluded from the officer ranks—with the notable exception of Oliver Cromwell. Soldiers were full-time paid professionals, instructed, drilled, subject to military discipline, and led by officers appointed and promoted on the basis of ability and experience rather than birth.

In June 1645 the New Model Army, with infantry under Sir Thomas Fairfax and a six-thousand-strong cavalry commanded by Cromwell, met Prince Rupert and the king's main army again, some twenty miles south of Leicester in the Battle of Naseby. It was the Royalist disaster that effectively determined the war's outcome. King Charles lost his infantry, arms, stores, and personal baggage, suffering six thousand casualties of seventy-four hundred combatants. The New Model Army's forces of fourteen thousand were left with four hundred killed or wounded.

When the professional New Model Army had finished its job in 1651 at the Battle of Worcester, Cromwell returned to London, acclaimed by the Rump Parliament as the only individual who could lead the country (and control the army).

As a head of government and chief executive officer, Oliver Cromwell didn't know what he was doing. How could he? England was now a republic, a commonwealth, but what did that mean? If England or any country in Europe had never been without a monarch, Cromwell certainly had no desire to be one. He, too, had done his job, and longed for nothing more than to return to his family and life as a country gentleman. As it had been throughout his years of service, however, Cromwell was motivated by his faith and his conviction that God had called him to his work.

So Cromwell turned his hand to administer the government of the new republic. In time he was named Lord Protector of the Commonwealth, and, ironically, exercised more unfettered executive powers than any king had ever effected. It was an executive of trial and error. On the whole, however, historians adjudge that Cromwell did an effective job as an administrator promoting civic justice and restoring the nation's reputation in Europe. Certainly, he was a far more pragmatic than ideological governor.

The Puritan Commonwealth has been easy to lampoon, but Cromwell and his peers were far from the dour pietists they are often portrayed as. Cromwell smoked a pipe, enjoyed sherry and his beer, loved to laugh and play games. His administration actively practiced toleration of religious practice. Even Catholics were allowed their freedom of worship, and Cromwell was a friend of George Fox, founder of the Quakers. A man of little personal vanity, Cromwell famously insisted that his portraits be painted "warts and all."

In September 1658 Cromwell died at age fifty-nine. Cromwell's reputation has ebbed and flowed in the centuries since his time. Hero or villain, however, Oliver Cromwell was one of the most significant figures in English history.

ointment. Parliament wanted to thank the army and send them home, but without being paid off, the restive army declined to disperse and leave London.

The only individual who had the respect of, standing with, and personal capacity to handle the New Model Army was Oliver Cromwell. While Cromwell's own expressed will was a desire to return to a quiet life in East Anglia, he was a natural leader who knew how to take command. And he was an elected member of Parliament, and one who signed the warrant for the king's execution. In fairly short order, that's how Cromwell came to be named chief executive, eventually designated Lord Protector, by the residual Parliament. In his turn, Cromwell made use of the officer corps in his organization of civil administration under the Commonwealth.

CHAPTER 10

The Accidental Commonwealth

The past is a foreign country; they do things differently there.
—L. P. HARTLEY

THE COMMONWEALTH'S IMPACT ON THE YOUNG COLONIES

The end of the Civil War meant the complete collapse of the Royalist cause. As the Stuart royal family fled to exile in France and Italy, the entourage included both of King Charles's sons. The eldest was now an uncrowned King Charles II; the younger, James, the Duke of York. Around them gathered a diminished court—the small circle of nobles and royal retainers that fled the Puritan Commonwealth with them.

In Virginia, however, the loyal Governor Berkeley engaged in an active campaign for the settlement of Royalists in the struggling colony. He advertised Virginia as "the last refuge of Royalists." Again, it was a wildly successful strategy. Through the active war years and through the 1650s as the Puritan Commonwealth unfolded, dozens of Royalist families staked their fortune in colonial Virginia. They did not come as small-time settlers, but to claim large parcels of Virginia Tidewater as plantations. They brought with them retainers and indentured servants to work the land and build the plantation houses, outbuildings, and towns.

It had taken thirty years for Virginia to reach a population of eight thousand—and ultimately sustainability as a colony. In the 1640s and 1650s, however, Virginia boomed in population and prosperity. Once again, Governor Berkeley had evidenced his political skills when the power in Westminster turned Puritan. He lay low at his plantation, Greenspring, when it was politic, but maintained his alliances and reputation with Virginia's leaders.

In New England, of course, the sympathies of Massachusetts Bay and its growing neighbors were with Parliament and the Puritan cause. The solidarity of the New England colonists was both political and religious. Though it would have been difficult to articulate this at the time, the "cause" of the Civil War reflected that entirely new Protestant worldview—what intellectual historians call a Weltanshauung. They shared in the joy and the optimism at an end to the Civil War, and in the triumph of their mutual cause.

For New England, it was a time of consolidation, stability, and relative prosperity. Settlements became communities, erected town houses, and gathered Congregational churches. Family followed family to the New World; a slow, but steady stream of like-minded new settlers arrived; regular commerce developed and Boston became a bustling harbor town.

Apart from the commonality of their English nationality, perhaps the most significant trait that they shared was their intolerance.

The two societies emerging in the English colonies of the New World in the mid-seventeenth century could scarcely have been more different. It may seem ironic from our twenty-first-century perspective, but apart from the commonality of their English nationality, perhaps the most significant trait that they shared was their intolerance. War might have been over in England, but that hardly meant a reconciliation of very different visions of human nature, society, human relationships, religion, and the institutions that embody them.

In Massachusetts Bay, there was certainly no separation of church and state. While the emerging egalitarian society of the Puritan and Reformed thinkers gave way to a very grassroots democracy in New

The Pull of the Homeland

In the Great Migration of the 1630s, the coastal towns of New England from Maine to New Haven were settled by Puritans seeking godly government and freedom of worship. The end of the Civil War and the establishment of the Puritan Commonwealth was an answer to their prayers. For virtually exiled Puritan pastors and others coerced to flee their vestries and villages, the door was open to return. The New World with its dangers, harsh climate, and deprivations did not become "home" for everyone, and many longed for the familiar gentle landscapes, families, and the relative comforts left behind. It is estimated that through the war and Commonwealth as many as a quarter of those who emigrated in the Great Migration pulled up stakes and sailed back for England.

England communities, participation in that democracy was restricted to members of the church. And church membership was no light matter. An individual had to give evidence of the work of grace in their life and submit to an examination by elders. Doctrinal soundness was a must.

In Virginia, on the other hand, the only church allowed in the fledgling colony was the established Church of England. Not only were other churches not permitted, but Sunday attendance at the parish Anglican Church was required by law. It wasn't until 1702 that something other than the established English church was legal in the colony.

THOSE CRAZY PURITAN COMMONWEALTH YEARS

Through the years of the 1650s, the Commonwealth actually worked far better than popular history usually gives it credit for—particularly considering the significant reality that it had no historical precedence in Western civilization, or really any body of political philosophy on which to draw. This is still more than a generation before what we call "the Enlightenment" and the emergence of the political theory that would undergird the arguments in the colonies for independence and a whole new form

Enter the Westminster Confession

The hot-blooded convictions of the Puritan Parliament were hardly uniform. There were Presbyterians and Independents (Congregationalists), Baptists, and those still in the Church of England. What united them, however, was a conviction that the English church required systemic reform and doctrinal clarity.

Despite the divergence of doctrinal and ecclesiastical views that emerged during the English Reformation, the notion that all these different versions of Christian faith and the churches they inspired could exist side by side and in civil and Christian harmony really hadn't been invented yet. Through the 1600s, it was largely just assumed that there was by natural and divine law an unbreakable connection between church and state, and that a state church was simply the order of things.

As relations between the King and Parliament had irrevocably broken down into war, in 1643 the House of Commons appointed an assembly of 151 theologians, academics, and clerics to tackle the problem and submit to Parliament a confession of faith and ecclesiastical practice that would accomplish just that. The commissioned assembly met 1,163 times over the next several years, in the crisis atmosphere of civil war, finally concluding in 1646. The Confession of Faith and Longer and Shorter Catechisms that they produced were each presented to and approved by Parliament in 1648. By the time the commission had completed its work, however, the House had fractured between Presbyterians and Independents and in practice the Westminster Confession of Faith ultimately never did become the defining doctrinal statement of the Church of England. Needless to say, the king and church episcopacy would have none of it.

of federal government. John Locke's *Two Treaties on Government* and An Essay *Concerning Human Understanding* in 1689 were seminal works that came too late to aid the guiding hands of the Commonwealth.

In practice, Oliver Cromwell consolidated more real political authority to himself and to his office of Lord Protector than the hapless Stuart kings ever enjoyed. Nevertheless, Cromwell was a highly devout man, who saw the world in the context of his times, and saw his role in it as one of responsibility and duty to God.

Somewhat ironically, though, the Westminster Confession became the most influential confession of Reformed Protestant theology ever composed. In 1647 the Scottish General Assembly adopted the Confession for the Kirk, replacing John Knox's Scots Confession of 1560 and the Heidelberg Catechism. It was ratified by the Scottish Parliament in 1649.

During the Commonwealth, the split between Presbyterians and Independents became sharper and clearly defined. It became obvious that the Westminster Confession would never govern the English church. In October 1658 a delegation of some two hundred pastors and elders from Congregational churches gathered at the Savoy Palace in London to affirm their own confession of faith. What they affirmed was largely the Westminster Confession. Their principal doctrinal alteration was the affirmation of Congregational polity—the spiritual and political independence of each congregation. This Savoy Declaration was reinforced by an essay in the preface titled "Of the Institution of Churches, and the Order Appointed in Them by Jesus Christ."

While there was no governing body or formal organization to adopt such creeds and confessions in New England, the Westminster Confession, modified by the Savoy Declaration, became the de facto doctrinal statement of the New England Puritans. Coming into the Middle Atlantic colonies with the Scotch-Irish Presbyterians, it became the confession of the first Presbyterian synod organized in the colonies in 1729. Subsequently, Presbyterians and Congregationalists agreed to recognize each other and respect each other's territory. That's why you don't see many old Presbyterian churches in New England, and Congregational churches are a rarity south of New York.

Cromwell was also street savvy, and he knew the hearts and minds of the officers that served under him through the Civil War. While the Commons continued to sit as the legislative branch of government (in rather abbreviated form), Oliver Cromwell used his knowledge of military organization and the talent that he knew from the New Model Army as the administrative arm of civil government. He divided the country into what were in essence military prefectures and appointed a military governor with the rank or title of major general. This, of course, is the derivation of Gilbert & Sullivan's famous Modern Major General satirized in *The Pirates of Penzance*. Once more, as it was in the New Model Army, the Puritan administration of Cromwell chose leaders on the basis of merit rather than birth.

The Puritans adjudged adultery to be a greater sin than murder—because adultery gave pleasure to two people and murder only to one.

Much has been scornfully written about the restrictive, joyless life of the Puritans, especially under the pious Parliamentarians who were making the rules. Again, with no concept of the separation of church and state, the goal of the Puritan state was to build a society consistent with their own conception of God's law. While the Commonwealth may not have been a theocracy, it certainly saw its duty as enforcing a Biblical life as they perceived it. The government imposed strict Sabbatarian laws (the source of the now antiquated "Blue Laws"), closed the theaters, banned public entertainments as frivolous, and so forth.

It was said that the Puritans banned bear baiting, not because it gave pain to the bear, but because it gave pleasure to the spectators. Another quip reckoned that the Puritans adjudged adultery to be a greater sin than murder—because adultery gave pleasure to two people and murder only to one. Undoubtedly, after living in the twenty-first-century world, no matter how devout we might be, we would find a Puritan society quite a struggle. Of course, the old saw about walking a mile in another's moccasins applies here as well. It's impossible to judge either the motives or the emotive reactions of those in past centuries.

The flame of sheer intellectual novelty and the "whole new world" wonder of the Reformation that came back from Europe in the late 1500s was still burning two and three generations later in the 1650s. But not surprisingly, it was beginning to burn progressively cooler.

For all the impositions upon the broader populace that the Puritan Parliament placed in the name of God, the Commonwealth was quite tolerant of dissent. In Puritan Massachusetts and the emergent colonies in New Hampshire and Connecticut, the "New England Way" was religiously exclusionary throughout the 1650s. Back in England, however, the prominent role of Dissenting (i.e., "Independent") clergy and gentry in the Parliamentary struggle, while the established state church episcopacy still existed, ensured in practice a measure of religious freedom in England.

CROMWELL AND IRELAND

Among Oliver Cromwell's uses for the army early in the Commonwealth was an invasion of Ireland. Troublesome though the island always was for England, Ireland had been subject to English overlordship for centuries. Unlike England, Ireland remained staunchly Roman Catholic through the sixteenth-century Reformation that eventually brought Protestantism to England. Inevitably, religious tensions contributed to the resentment the Irish felt for English feudal dominance.

Since an Irish rebellion in 1641, most of Ireland had been controlled by the Irish Catholic Confederation. An alliance was signed in 1649 between the Confederate Catholics and Charles II (now in exile in France) and English Royalists. Royalist troops flowed to Ireland and the Irish Confederate Catholic troops were placed under the command of Royalist officers led by James Butler, the Earl of Ormande. Their avowed aim was to invade England and restore the Stuart monarchy. It was an active threat that the new Puritan Commonwealth could not afford to ignore.

In August 1649 the English Rump Parliament sent the New Model Army to Ireland under the command of Oliver Cromwell. The only remaining Parliamentarian outpost in Ireland at the time was the capitol of Dublin. A combined Royalist/Confederate force under Ormande moved at Rathmines, south of the city, to take Dublin and deprive Cromwell of a landing port. The commanding colonel, Michael Jones, however, routed the Royalists in a surprise attack, killing some four thousand coalition soldiers and taking twenty-five hundred prisoners. It meant the

Parliamentarians had a secure port at which to land their army. Cromwell arrived with thirty-five ships of troops and equipment on August 15th; Gen. Henry Ireton landed two days later with another seventy-seven ships.

Ormonde's troops retreated from around Dublin in disarray. Badly demoralized by their unexpected defeat at Rathmines, they were rendered incapable of fighting another pitched battle. In a series of small battles and skirmishes the New Model Army always prevailed. By October of 1650 the Parliamentarians had chased them across the Shannon into the western province of Connacht. Discredited by a constant stream of defeats, Ormonde fled for France in December 1650 and was replaced as commander by an Irish nobleman, Ulick Burke of Clanricarde.

Penned west of the River Shannon, however, Irish and Royalist coalition forces placed their last hope on defending the strongly walled cities of Limerick and Galway. Ireton besieged Limerick while Charles Coote surrounded Galway. Unable to take the fortified cities by assault, they blockaded them until hunger and disease forced surrender. Limerick fell in 1651 and Galway the following year. Disease killed on both sides of the walls, however, and the great Civil War general Henry Ireton died of plague outside Limerick in 1651, along with thousands of his troops.

Estimates conclude that fifty thousand people, many prisoners of war, were deported as indentured laborers to the English colonies in America and the West Indies.

The fall of Galway saw the end of organized resistance to the Cromwellian conquest, but Irish troops continued to launch guerilla attacks on the New Model Army. At the end of 1651 there were still estimated to be thirty thousand men in arms against the Parliamentarians. English reprisals systematically destroyed food stocks in several counties, resulting in famine through much of the country. The outbreak of bubonic plague added millions of deaths. Estimates conclude that fifty thousand people, many prisoners of war, were deported as indentured laborers to the English colonies in America and the West Indies. Ireland was pacified, but at a terrible cost.

With Ireland secure in Protestant hands, the northwestern province of the island, the ancient Celtic kingdom of Ulster, became inviting territory for emigration across the Irish Sea from the Scottish lowlands and the border country.

The southern Scottish counties of Dumfries and Galloway and the Borders had been a lawless country for centuries, punctuated by generations of border raids, family feuds, and what we would call "frontier justice." For Scots from that rough-and-tumble, often violent, culture, Ulster's poor Celtic populace held no fear. Sparsely populated and fertile for farming, Ulster became the destination for a generation of Scottish economic migrants, bringing their own Presbyterian faith into a hitherto Catholic island.

THE CROWN: DENIED AND REGAINED

Several times through the 1650s Cromwell was offered the English crown, and he consistently refused to accept it. That Parliament offered the monarchy to his hands reflects a measure of the uncertainty with which they governed. After all, among the chief duties of kings for generations had been to provide for a succession. Through Cromwell's government in the 1650s, no "heir apparent" emerged as a natural successor—and no mechanism existed in the thinking of Parliament to provide one.

Oliver Cromwell died in 1658. Having been urged to designate his own successor, Cromwell, naturally enough, at last named his son, Richard. Alas, as so often happens, the son did not possess the leadership abilities and political sophistication of the father. In fairly short order, the Puritan Commonwealth began to unravel. The ideology and the huge shift in worldview introduced by the Puritan Reformation remained in churches, the universities, and in the marketplace of ideas. The religious fervor that motivated so many through the years before, during, and after the Civil War, however, was simply a spent force. Sooner or later, religious fervor always wanes.

Besides, ordinary English folk were tired of the strictures of life under the Puritans and of the uncertainties that government by Parliament and a weak executive continued to project.

In 1660 a deputation led by Gen. Monk invited Charles I's son to return from exile in France and take the united throne of England, Scotland, and Ireland. Charles II's triumphant return to London and coronation was not without conditions, however. Covenants assured that King Charles II would not rule on his own, but under the direction of Parliament. There was to be a Restoration, but it was to be a limited monarchy. Charles II was only too happy to agree. The experiment of the Puritan Commonwealth was over.

CHAPTER 11

Restoration of the Stuart Monarchy

The worst of revolutions is restoration.

—CHARLES JAMES FOX

SOCIOLOGISTS AND HISTORIANS OF SOCIETY HAVE OFTEN OBSERVED HOW the pendulum of civic fashion swings from the conventional and staid to the exuberant and bound breaking. And back again. From the rigorous enthusiasms of the rising Puritan voice over a period of two generations, English society was about to embark on a few wild decades of reaction. Once again, what happened in the court of King Charles II, in Parliament, and on the streets of London would stamp an indelible character on the colonies across the Atlantic.

THE WHEEL TURNS AGAIN

The sentiment of the mob is always a fickle thing. In a decade, the London populace went from cheering for the execution of the king to cheering the arrival of his son in full regal splendor. The vociferous support the crowd gave the Puritan Parliament through the tensions of the 1640s became equally as frenzied shaking off the rigors of the Puritan society. Those MPs still living who had signed the warrant for regicide were attainted as traitors and executed. The body of Oliver Cromwell (among others) was exhumed and dragged through the streets in disgrace.

There was celebration at Charles's coronation—the beginning of a party that would go on for years. It became, simply, the Restoration. Through the 1660s the theaters were opened, public entertainments were reestablished, music flourished, and the repressive Sabbath laws were abolished. Life returned to what folks thought back on nostalgically as "normal."

The Puritans were out, and the Royalists were back in. The Restoration of the monarchy meant the restoration of the court. The remnant of ancient landed nobility, who had supported the king through the Civil War and waited silently through the exile of the Stuart heir, returned to court—a cadre of festive peers ready to celebrate.

The relationship between the monarch and Parliament had altered measurably and forever, however. King Charles II had no objections to the conditions that Parliament laid down for his triumphal return. As it turned out, Charles II had little inclination to involve himself in government at all. Perfectly content to let his ministers and Parliament manage the affairs of state, Charles II and his inner circle were quite happy to enjoy the spoils of victory and the majesty of monarchy.

In fact, they captured the mood of the country and set the example in that national celebration. The court became a model of licentiousness and a hedonistic lifestyle. London and the aristocracy followed suit. Playwrights of the day, such as William Congreve, William Wycherly, George Etheridge, and others, filled the London theaters with what became known as Restoration comedy, as ribald and daring as you'll find on the West End today, and the theatrical progenitor of the English bedroom farce. Charles II became known for his mistresses—and his illegitimate children. Poet John Dryden in his 1681 "Absalom and Achitophel" famously satirized the king as having "scattered his Maker's image o'er the land." No wonder he was known as the "Merry Monarch."

Out in the provinces and market towns, there were still plenty of pious Puritans, but their ascendancy had passed. The national mood, and certainly that of an aristocracy and landed nobility that had survived the war and Commonwealth, was in no spirit for serious religion.

The Achilles' heel of the Royal Stuart family was still religion.

The Restoration of the Stuart monarchy in the 1660s was the first time in history (and one of the few) when a toppled royal dynasty was successfully restored to the throne. Alas, its success and the Stuart dynasty were to be short-lived. The Achilles' heel of the Royal Stuart family was still religion.

The practical settlement for the Church of England was pragmatic rather than principled. Most people were just tired of fighting about it. The Westminster Confession was by and large conveniently forgotten in the established church, and little by little the Church settled into an inclusive identity based upon a unity of practice, polity, and liturgy rather than a unity of doctrine. There emerged three distinct branches of the Church that have coexisted since the turn of the eighteenth century, whose unity has really only been threatened in the last few years with the highly publicized controversies over such issues as homosexuality and female ordination.

At its most conservative, the Anglo-Catholic branch of Anglicanism can claim the purest descent from the church that King Henry VIII conceived when he broke with Rome and the Pope. They maintain many more of the forms and customs of Roman Catholicism than other branches of the Protestant family tree. Worship is highly liturgical, and the Eucharist plays a bigger and more solemn role in the service.

The "Low Church" or evangelical wing of the Church descends from the Puritans that remained within the established church. Worship is less formal; the sermon is more important; the Bible is more important than the Book of Common Prayer; and there is the Reformation emphasis upon personal faith.

By far the largest and most influential party that emerged with the Restoration church, however, became the "Broad Church." In a sense, these were the folks that just didn't care that much. They still believed in going to church, and in a Protestant, national Church of England. After a century of high seriousness, bloodshed, and ecclesiastical contention, though, a good majority were just happy to go with the flow, and not take religion too seriously.

Through the century that followed, the Church became a respected profession for the younger sons of gentlemen. If the oldest son inherited

John Bunyan and *The Pilgrim's Progress*

The Restoration brought with it the legal demand once again that control of worship belonged to the Church. John Bunyan, son of a poor tinker from Bedfordshire, attended a local grammar school and mustered into the Parliamentary army during the Civil War. He gradually converted to Puritanism during the 1650s and became a skilled lay preacher. With the Restoration, in 1661 the local assize court sent him to prison for holding services not conforming to the Church of England. Ultimately, Bunyan suffered two imprisonments totaling more than twelve years, during which time he wrote several books. Though formally uneducated much beyond literacy, he proved a skillful and imaginative writer. During his latter stint in jail, Bunyan penned *The Pilgrim's Progress.*

The statue commemorating John Bunyan stands at the corner of the park at the center of Bedford just a few blocks from the Bunyan Meeting, an active Congregational church that dates from 1650.

A Christian allegory that details the journey of Pilgrim through life, as its full title continues, "From this world to that which is come," *The Pilgrim's Progress* was first published in 1678 and became something of an instant hit. The book went through several editions in the next few years and was first published in Massachusetts in 1681. It soon became "required" reading, present in most New England homes.

What became among the most influential books of all time, *The Pilgrim's Progress* has never been out of print from its first publication to now. It has been translated into some two hundred languages.

the landed estates and titles, the younger sons had to do something. Along with law and the military, holy orders were the respectable way. Religious conviction as such often had little to do with it.

HOW THE WHEEL TURNED THE NEW WORLD

The wheel that turned in England turned in its New World colonies as well. Now, it was New England's share to be the one remaining Puritan refuge, where an intentional society still pursued that "city on a hill" and a godly community. Outward migration from England increased and new settlements continued to grow from seacoast New Hampshire to south along Long Island Sound.

Virginia thrived. The roots planted by wealthy, aristocratic Royalists along the Tidewater and spreading inland in great plantations paid off. With the Restoration of the monarchy, through the late decades of the 1600s the tobacco trade with England became highly profitable. Jamestown strived to become a fashionable colonial capital and getting in on spacious land grants for propertied gentlemen became all the rage. Berkeley's campaign to attract wealthy Royalists continued. Most of those families that became the "First Families of Virginia"—the Carrs and the Carters, Washingtons and Fairfaxes—arrived in the colony between 1645 and 1665.

EXTENDING THE ROYALIST SOUTH

In 1663 King Charles II extended the Royalist South, chartering the province of Carolina, named in honor of his father, to a group of eight loyal friends designated as Lords Proprietors. It was not until 1670, though, that their expeditions to take possession of the new colony resulted in the settlement of Charleston—Charles Town, named for King Charles II himself.

Capital of the colony from the beginning, Charleston quickly became a port of inward migration. Plantation settlements spread through the low country. While most of the earliest settlers were British, they came not only from England, but from Bermuda and Barbados as well. Many of them brought African laborers, many of them enslaved. As the staging and supply depot for settlement of Carolina, Charleston grew quickly, becoming one of the largest towns and most prosperous ports in the colonies by 1690.

Early on, the Proprietors appointed a deputy governor for the large region north of Cape Fear. Back in London, the Lords Proprietors formally divided their colony into North and South Carolina in 1710. Together, however, the Carolinas at that time had a settler population estimated at only about ten thousand.

BACON'S REBELLION AND KING PHILIP'S WAR

The last threat to Virginia's colonial integrity proved the last challenge for Governor William Berkeley. In 1675 the colony was hit by a drought that ravaged agricultural crops, including the tobacco that was the farmers' cash crop. Anxiety and unrest swept the colony. In 1676 hundreds of frontiersmen rallied behind one Nathaniel Bacon, who led attacks against neighboring Indian tribes, unfortunately not all of them previously hostile. Berkeley condemned rather than commissioned Bacon, and a virtual civil war ensued.

In September 1676 Bacon and his followers laid siege to Jamestown, forced Berkeley to flee the town, and burned the capital to the ground. When Bacon died of dysentery the next month, Bacon's Rebellion petered out. Within a few months, Berkeley had hunted down and hanged many of the rebellion's leaders and resumed control of the colony. Sir William Berkeley died in 1677, after thirty-five years as Virginia's colonial governor.

While Governor Berkeley and Virginia were occupied with civil rebellion and its aftermath, the New England colonies faced their first widespread, organized Indian uprising that was known as King Philip's War. The eponymous King Philip was the son of Massasoit, the Wampanoag chief. Unlike his father, he did not have good relations with the English immigrants. A series of incidents in the early 1670s, however, including boycotting trade with the Indians, an attempt to disarm them, and finally the judicial hanging of several Wampanoag in Plymouth in 1675 enflamed Philip (by his Indian name, Metacom) to launch a spreading assault with a growing base of tribal allies across the settled New England colonies.

Over the next year and a half, there were Indian attacks on settled communities from the coast of Maine to the western Massachusetts towns of the Connecticut River Valley and throughout eastern Massachusetts and Rhode Island. A New England Confederation was formed in September 1675 to meet the threat with a united front and a declaration of war against the aggressing tribes.

By the next summer, however, fifty-two—more than half—of the New England towns had been attacked, with twelve completely destroyed—predominantly in southeastern Massachusetts and Rhode Island. Raids, ambushes, sieges and torture, execution of captives, and indentured servitude were all the rage—on both sides.

Very quickly, however, towns along the Connecticut River fortified. Each town's perfunctory militia organized and banded together under elected officers. Lines of communication and aid weaved the colonial towns together in a united war effort. Soon, skirmishes and Indian attacks began to turn to English successes, and Indian deaths.

The English citizens of each of the several colonies also began to share a common identity and a mutual aid system that would emerge again in the decades to come.

By the summer of 1676, Indians began surrendering to the colonials. Metacom was run to ground by a raiding party in a swamp south of Providence. He was duly shot and killed in what might be called a spontaneous execution. His head, however, was brought home as a trophy and placed on display in Plymouth for years. With the death of its titular leader, King Philip's War was effectively over. Active warfare continued sporadically along the Maine coast's inlets and rivers north to Penobscot Bay until 1678.

In its impact upon the colonies involved, King Philip's War was the deadliest and most destructive in our colonial history.

In its impact upon the colonies involved, King Philip's War was the deadliest and most destructive in our colonial history. Thousands of deaths left thousands of broken families in small communities and thousands of rural farmsteads destroyed or seriously damaged. The New England Puritans were resilient, but it took many years to rebuild and renew their lives, livelihoods, and communities.

For many of the defeated tribes and subtribes of the dwindling native Indians, however, King Philip's War was annihilating. Only an estimated four hundred Wampanoag survived the war, and they virtually disappeared as a tribe. In many instances, Indian captives were sold into slavery in the Caribbean or Spain. Throughout south-central New England, there were not enough indigenous Indians remaining to pose an organized threat again.

A Hybrid Colony in the Mid-Atlantic

When the English captured and held the small New Netherlands colony centered around New Amsterdam on lower Manhattan island in 1664, they acquired with it a significant portion on the west side of the Hudson River in what would become New Jersey. The Dutch, however, were not the only people attempting to colonize the region.

Swedes established a settlement in southwestern New Jersey along the east bank of the Delaware River—appropriately named New Sweden. It numbered some four hundred colonists by 1655 when the Dutch sent down a regiment of soldiers and annexed the fledgling colony. That then, too, became British territory a decade later.

A restored King Charles II gave the region between the New England colonies and Maryland as a proprietary grant to his brother, James, the Duke of York. The area between the Hudson and Delaware Rivers, King Charles named New Jersey after the Channel Island that had given him hospitality during his Commonwealth exile. In the 1680s King James II granted New Jersey to two loyal friends, Sir George Carteret and Lord John Berkeley, the older brother of Sir William Berkeley. When Lord Berkeley sold his portion to the Quakers in 1674, the colony became divided into East and West Jersey. They were united again as a royal possession in 1702 by then Queen Anne. Though New York and New Jersey squabbled over the border between them for decades, New Jersey was finally defined as an independent colony.

CHAPTER 12

William Penn and the Middle Way

True godliness does not turn men out of the world, but enables them to live better in it and excites their endeavors to mend it.
—WILLIAM PENN

THE QUAKERS FIND A MIDDLE WAY

As bad a rap as the Puritan Commonwealth received, and perhaps deserved, they also brought a relief from the religious persecution that had characterized a full century of English life before them. From the time in the 1530s when Henry VIII began executing people for contesting his ecclesiastical wavering, England had been in a constant state of religious strife. The Dissenters had been on the receiving end of that for more than a generation, largely for being Nonconformists. With the control of Parliament in the hands of Dissenters, Independents, and Presbyterians alike, the pursuit and persecution of Nonconformists ceased. As anathematic as Catholicism was, in fact, even practicing Catholics were left undisturbed (and generally had the good sense to keep their heads down).

The Restoration of the monarchy, however, brought the restoration of the church. Though it evolved into a very Broad Church indeed, the national church was back—and woe once again fell upon those whose convictions took them in a different direction. Conformity to the Anglican Church was once again the law of the land.

Among the many individuals whose consciences, imaginations, and scholarship took them outside the church was George Fox. Fox pursued spirituality and Biblical truth in a different direction altogether. He saw individual responsibility and equality much more broadly than even the Puritans—with a Holy Spirit that directly illumined the Scriptures and the soul without need of teachers or the formalization of traditional worship, let alone liturgy.

Out of a northern background with few credentials to his name, Fox gathered around himself those who would have been considered "radical Reformationists" in their day. Led by the "inner light" that they trusted, their quiet worship and introspective inspiration brought such ecstasies that they trembled in their public worship of the Lord. Wags called George Fox's followers "Quakers."

Quakers fit nowhere in what had become the traditional spectrum of English religious conviction. They were convicted to follow Jesus in a far different way than even seventeenth-century society expected. Among other things, they followed the Sermon on the Mount literally—turn the other cheek meant just that. The Quakers were pacifist, distaining physical violence not just in martial conflict but in domestic life as well. Yes, this was radical. Quakers genuinely believed in human equality, and thus declined to pay obeisance to human assignments of social status. In practical terms, they didn't observe the social fineries of groveling before one's betters. They would not doff their cap to the lord of the manor, or bow in the presence of nobility, or swear an oath of allegiance or before a court.

Wanting to worship outside the organization of the national church was one thing. Thumbing one's institutional nose at the centuries-old mores of the social order was quite something else entirely. Industrious, humble, and intrinsically nonrevolutionary by nature, the Quakers became a subject of persecution under the restored Church of England in the 1660s and 1670s.

Among George Fox's early and most prominent followers was William Penn. This was not an inconsiderable man. Yes, indeed, Penn was a Quaker, who somehow got this land grant and built Philadelphia, the "City of Brotherly Love" and there's a state named after him. Thus endeth the lesson in American lore, but it wasn't quite as simple as that.

William Penn was the well-connected son of an English admiral. His father, Admiral William Penn, had served Parliament and Oliver Cromwell through the Civil War, and was rewarded with huge landed estates in Ireland that had been confiscated by Cromwell on his subjugation of the Irish revolt in support of the Stuarts. The younger Penn grew up in the Commonwealth, was well schooled, and was eventually sent off to Oxford. After the death of Cromwell, however, the elder Penn's sentiments changed with many others, and he supported the Restoration of the monarchy. In fact, Admiral Penn was sent to France to bring Charles II and his family back to England. For his part in the Restoration, the admiral was knighted.

This was going to be a very different colony, and its geographical location— lying between the New England Congregationalists and the Southern Anglican Royalists—would result in a historical importance for the colony that Penn could have little predicted.

While being tutored on the family plot in Ireland, the younger Penn was introduced to the Quaker teachings of Fox. It wasn't until several years later, while he was at Christ Church, Oxford, in the heady years of the early 1660s, however, that Penn's religious focus sharpened to the Quaker cause.

Penn became a leading Quaker preacher, theologian, and spokesman, traveling with Fox across England and to Europe, and authoring tracts in defense of Quaker belief. He even did a couple of stints in prison because of his beliefs. Penn's prominence ultimately protected him, and his connections paid off. At one point, much to Penn's chagrin, his father directly intervened, paying a fine and bailing him out of prison. Ultimately, the death of Admiral Penn brought an end to the political protection his prominence provided the younger William. At the same time, the pressure of Conformity was more than a passing annoyance to beleaguered Quakers.

THE GRANT OF PENN'S WOODS

The best solution for Quakers increasingly seemed to be to leave England. In fact, they began by purchasing large tracts of what is now southern New Jersey. Following that lead, in 1681 Penn persuaded King Charles II to settle an old debt to his father by giving him a New World land grant. As Charles saw it, this cost him little; Penn saw the opportunity to create a refuge for Quakers. Penn called his new colony "Sylvania"—Latin for woods or forest. It was King Charles II himself who consequently called the grant Pennsylvania, in honor of the late admiral.

Unlike Massachusetts Bay or Virginia, but like New Hampshire, Carolina, and Maryland, "Penn's Woods" was a proprietary colony—the largest in the American colonies. Penn himself drew up its charter of governance, the plans for its capital town, and the scheme for its settlement. This was going to be a very different colony, and its geographical location—lying between the New England Congregationalists and the Southern Anglican Royalists—would result in a historical importance for the colony that Penn could have little predicted.

William Penn must have had a good deal of fun in 1681 drawing up the blueprints for a new society based upon Quaker principles. After all, he was the "sovereign" of his colony, and not many individuals, then or now, get to sit down and plan what was virtually a nation, or at least a city-state.

In England at the time, there were some two hundred capital crimes—crimes liable to receive the death penalty. In Penn's new colony, there were

"Admiral Penn's Woods"

It's a bar bet worth remembering. Who was the Commonwealth of Pennsylvania named for? The answer, of course, is the famous William Penn's father, Admiral William Penn—and named so by none other than King Charles II, who gave the eponymous son the huge proprietary land grant.

only two capital crimes: treason and murder. There would not be religious restrictions on citizenship or office, and each individual was recognized as equal before the law, as before God. Many of the fundamental precepts of society that we take for granted today got their beginning in this country with Penn's original design for Pennsylvania, and were radical—even unheard of—in his day.

By 1682 Penn was confident enough in his planning to send out to what became Philadelphia the first ship of Quaker colonists. Among the passengers were strangers to the English Quakers. Aboard the *Nautilus* were thirteen families of German Mennonites. They were there on Penn's explicit invitation.

While the Quakers were suffering under pressure to conform in England, Anabaptists in the Alsace and German Rhineland low country were being persecuted for many of the same beliefs that caused the Quakers such hardship in England—a belief in the primacy of individual conscience, nonviolence, turning the other cheek, and, by Christ's example, to be no respecter of persons' rank or economic station. Those German Anabaptists became the Mennonites, Amish, and Brethren we know today as "Pennsylvania Dutch." It is, of course, an English corruption of the Pennsylvania *Deutsch*—the German Anabaptist community that is, in fact, the oldest European minority subculture in America.

The original Mennonite arrivals settled land Penn sold them in 1683, Germantown. They were joined by other families in the years to come and then by wave after wave of settlers between 1720 and 1770, from southwestern Germany, German Switzerland, Bohemia, and Moravia. They were Mennonites and Amish following the teaching of Menno Simons and his more conservative coreligionist Jacob Amiens. But they were also Lutheran, Quaker, Reformed, and Moravian as well. German communities settled (and still characterize) Lancaster County and the fertile farmland of south-central Pennsylvania. They spread west through Pennsylvania into Ohio and south across the neck of Maryland into northern Virginia and down the Shenandoah Valley. By the time of the Revolutionary War, more than half of Pennsylvania's population claimed German descent.

WHAT DID DELAWARE?

To New Jersey's south, separated by Delaware Bay, Delaware was similarly an area that evolved into a colony rather than was chartered or granted as such back in Britain—or anywhere else.

Swedish colonists had arrived in 1638 and established the first permanent settlement at Fort Christina, near present-day Wilmington. The Dutch came a dozen years later and built their own fortified village in New Castle. By the mid-1650s, the Dutch had absorbed control of the Swedes and incorporated the territory into their New Netherlands. Of course, the Dutch didn't hold it for long as New Netherlands was annexed by England in 1664.

Delaware was claimed by James, Duke of York (and later King James II), who directed the small flotilla that drove the Dutch from their New World stake. James in turn passed on his control to William Penn by lease in 1682. What were known as "the Lower Counties on the Delaware" provided Penn with a crucial avenue to the sea for his Pennsylvania province.

When Penn arrived in his proprietary colony that year, he established a representative assembly that included representatives from each county in Pennsylvania and the Lower Counties. As the "Upper Counties," and Philadelphia in particular, grew rapidly, the sparsely populated Lower Counties seemed increasingly out of the Pennsylvania loop. In 1704 the regions agreed to separate their legislative assemblies. While both colonies remained the proprietary possessions of Penn and his heirs, they shared governors for many years.

Though the new colony was actually named after the Delaware River, the river was named for Thomas West, 3rd Baron De La Warr, the first royal governor of the Colony of Virginia. Lord De La Warr had led the relief mission to Jamestown in 1610 after the terrible "starving time" of the 1609 winter. The state of Delaware is thus the only American state to be named for a colonial governor or member of the English nobility.

In a sense, William Penn was the man who made America. What the Quakers brought to the Delaware Valley that was lacking in either New England or Virginia's expanding sphere of influence was tolerance. The emergent Quaker communities in Philadelphia and expanding westward

The Mason-Dixon Line

William Penn's grant did not go unchallenged. Lord Baltimore, Cecil Calvert, claimed that his grant of Maryland included lands on the western side of Delaware Bay, which would encompass all of present Delaware. Their dispute (inherited by their heirs) resulted in decades of litigation in London's High Court of Chancery. In the early 1760s the Penns and Calverts eventually agreed to commission English surveyors Charles Mason and Jeremiah Dixon to survey the 233-mile border between Pennsylvania and Maryland, as well as the 83-mile border that parsed Delaware (still claimed by Penn's heirs) from Maryland.

The work of Mason and Dixon took almost five years to completion in 1767. The boundaries they established were marked in a fashion the English had used since it was brought by the Romans—with milestones, sometimes of considerable size. Every fifth mile, a "crownstone" was raised, engraved with the coats of arms of the Penn and Calvert families.

The resulting Mason-Dixon Line that defined three colonies came to be seen as demarcating the North and South and, soon, as the line between slave states and free states. Delaware, though on the northern side of the divide, was a slave state. Almost a century later, in the American Civil War, however, Delaware stayed with the Union and abolished slavery with the Emancipation Proclamation in 1863.

toward the Appalachians brought their intense personal spirituality, their familiar second-person pronouns (the "thee" and "thou" of the King James Bible) and their nonviolent convictions. They also brought with them an appreciation for their freedom from persecution for their beliefs.

The difference with Penn and the Quakers was that they determined not to impose on others the strictures of religious conformity that drove them from their English homes. The colony of Pennsylvania would not force folks to be Quaker; they would allow people the freedom (dare we say "right"?) to worship according to their own convictions. While that well may seem to be obvious to our twenty-first-century American sensibility, this was groundbreaking for them. In brief, the whole notion we think of as American, that people and churches have the right to worship according to the dictates of their conscience, found its first expression in this land in the proprietary colony of William Penn and his Quaker followers.

As the world veered toward the eighteenth century, most folk out in the provinces still believed in that meaningful, necessary, and desirable connection between the church and state. There may have remained huge differences in belief as to how that state church ought to be configured, both doctrinally and organizationally, but it was still largely believed that a unified people, a nation, should have a single church. In practice, the Quakers of Pennsylvania broke the mold.

The first two Great Migrations of the 1600s, the Puritans to New England in the 1630s and '40s and the Anglican Royalists to Virginia in the 1650s and '60s, had indelibly stamped their mark on the dynamic New World. The Quakers coming into the mid-Atlantic between them became the third Great Migration.

In England, meanwhile, there was yet another revolution brewing.

THE GLORIOUS REVOLUTION OF 1688

King Charles II died in 1685 without a legitimate heir. Charles may have scattered his Maker's image, but the seed never fell to secure the lineal succession. That left the British throne to his younger brother, James, who became King James II. Unhappily for Britain, James was a Catholic.

There was already rebellion against the Catholic succession. That summer, Charles II's illegitimate son, James Scott, the Protestant Duke of Monmouth, became the focal point for rebellion in the West Country. Admittedly, it was short-lived. A decisive battle on July 6, 1685, the Battle of Sedgemoor, put an end to the rebellion. The nighttime battle on the plains of Somerset was recorded in R. D. Blackmoor's romantic novel *Lorna Doone*.

Monmouth was taken to London and beheaded on Tower Hill. King Charles sent an emissary, Judge Jeffries, into the West Country to administer justice. His trials were termed the "Bloody Assizes," and hundreds were sent to the gallows or worse in Dorset and Devon. So much for Monmouth's Rebellion.

The insistent spirit of that uprising, that after more than a century of religious conflict, turmoil, and disquiet a Protestant should occupy the throne of England, however, remained the overwhelming sentiment of the English people.

King James II made every kind of overture to convince the English Commons and Lords that he would indeed conform to the Anglican settlement that was now beginning to become almost normative in the shires, but he was fudging. His family was Catholic, and he had never hidden his own loyalties to the Roman Catholic faith. Not only were his own actions as monarch consistent with that faith, but the House of Commons still had to deal with the matter of succession.

Parliament established that, on behalf of the English people, it had the right to determine the individual that sat on the English throne.

Parliament did not have far to fish for an alternative to James. Just across the channel, Mary Stuart, granddaughter of Henry VII, was married to the Protestant Prince William of Orange in the ardently Reformed Calvinist Netherlands. After some negotiation, William agreed to come to England with his wife, Mary, but only on the understanding that they would reign as co-monarchs together. After some reluctance, Parliament agreed. In November 1688 William of Orange landed in Brixham, Devon, with a small contingent and proceeded to London.

King James II, meanwhile, was quietly deposed and shuffled, with his family, off to France. The events have long been called the Glorious Revolution. That nomenclature itself, of course, is yet another clear example of history being determined by the winner. The results were hardly considered "Glorious" by the Royal Stuarts or by their followers and supporters—particularly in Scotland, where despite their own strong Presbyterianism many still considered the Stuarts their own royal family.

Visiting the 1600s

It should not be surprising that the place where you can still find homes and buildings built in the 1600s is the New England coastline. A number of these are restored or preserved by Historic New England, which conserves thirty-six classic properties open to the public and provides tours (some only on weekends). Their seventeeth-century residences are concentrated from Boston north to Portsmouth.

The Spencer-Peirce-Little Farm in Newbury, Massachusetts, was built in 1690 as a country retreat for wealthy merchants from nearby Newburyport at the mouth of the Merrimack River. Designed and constructed, inside as well as out, quite as a country manor house would have been in the England of that day, the property is a National Historic Landmark. Today, the farm also fosters animals for the Massachusetts Society for the Prevention of Cruelty to Animals.

On the other hand, the results certainly were revolutionary. Parliament established that, on behalf of the English people, *it* had the right to determine the individual that sat on the English throne. The balance of power had incontrovertibly shifted from the monarch to the representative assembly of the people. The king and/or queen ruled not only in Parliament, but with Parliament's express permission. The result was the foundation of what we today term a limited, or constitutional, monarchy. What made this revolution of 1688 "Glorious," however, was not its political result, but because it was accomplished without bloodshed.

While history generally records the joint reign of William and Mary as happy and successful (ending with William III's death in 1704), not everyone was pleased with the settlement—or willing to take it peacefully.

CHAPTER 13

At the Turn of the Eighteenth Century

Perfect freedom is as necessary to the health and vigor of commerce as it is to the health and vigor of citizenship.

—PATRICK HENRY

IN 1700 THE POPULATION OF THE ENGLISH COLONIES IN NORTH AMERica numbered about 275,000. They were spread out along the Atlantic coast from the Province of Maine (a part of Massachusetts) to the thinly inhabited Carolinas. Most of the population lived in coastal towns. Beyond the immediate coast, in New England, small communities had formed along the navigable rivers like the Merrimack, the Housatonic, and the Connecticut. In the south, Chesapeake Bay afforded easy access for settlement of the Delmarva Peninsula and western rivers—the Rappahanock, the James, and the York.

North or south, however, towns and villages were unimaginably small by our frame of reference. In the north, a community of farm families and artisans might number eighty or a hundred people, located by water and occasionally dirt-track road a dozen miles or more from their nearest neighbors. In the Tidewater, the large plantations may have been neighbors, but town might be a two-hour ride by horse. Boston was the largest town, with a population of seven thousand—about that of today's Elkins, West Virginia, or Rockland, Maine. New York was the second city, with a population of five thousand.

There was now a continual stream of colonists coming from Britain. Whether they came as indentured servants, relatives of those already

Boston: Land of the Bean and the Cod

While seven thousand residents hardly seems like a good-sized town today, at the turn of the eighteenth century that made a sizable English city. London was a sprawling urban metropolis of an estimated four hundred thousand, but only a dozen cities in England were larger than Boston at the time. Boston was already playing above its weight with an economy equaling major English ports such as Bristol, Liverpool, and Hull, and the growing town had some swagger.

Tobacco drove the wealth in Virginia; in Boston it was fish—specifically Atlantic cod caught in the cold waters off the North Atlantic coast from Cape Ann to Newfoundland. Over the next decades, the number of cod caught, processed by curing or drying, and exported to Europe and the Caribbean steadily increased to more than twenty million a year. The fishing fleets returned to Boston laden with cargos of coffee, wine, molasses, spices, and other "luxury" commodities.

It had now been seventy years since Boston was settled as the Puritan "city on the hill." While public mores and laws remained largely unchanged, its rapid commercialization and international trade were eroding the hegemony of its strict homogeneity of Puritan belief and behavior. There were strangers in the streets, taverns, and growing neighborhoods.

In 1691 King William III altered Massachusetts's royal charter, changing the franchise qualification from church membership to property ownership. Status in Boston and soon throughout the colonial towns began to shift from standing within the local church to more material indicators. That is, wealth began to trump piety.

here, or religious migrants, however, they all came seeking greener pastures—literally.

For most folk making the dangerous, uncomfortable ocean crossing, taking their opportunity in the New World was the only way that they could dream of owning their own land, house, or business. The economic and social realities of life in Stuart England meant such freedom and social mobility, such economic aspiration, was not practically within the imagination for most. On the other hand, what the New World had was plenty of land—in fact, a limitless supply. In fact, no one knew how much.

In 1700 no one really knew what lay over that range of mountains to the west (there was always a range of mountains to the west). Today, on any of sundry devices, we can almost instantly access satellite images homing in at street level nearly anywhere on the globe. Regardless of how detailed our own knowledge of world geography is, it is difficult to imagine living in a world where most of that world is terra incognita for everyone. Though explorers had followed the Atlantic rivers, most of the inland was unknown. No one knew how far the continent stretched. Of course, that did not stop sundry kings, councils, and holders of proprietary charters from claiming it or parsing it out for settlement.

Then there were the indigenous peoples, the Indians. In the 1600s the Native Americans were equally an unknown commodity to English settlers. Once again, it's easy from our contemporary ethos to stand aghast at colonial (and subsequently American) dealings with the Native Americans.

The native tribal Indians, however, were something so totally other to Europeans that it was difficult to know what to make of them. In an era when many people didn't travel farther than twenty miles from their birthplace in their lives, there was a certain homogeneity in human experience. To most English folk living anywhere other than London, meeting someone from Austria would have been a remarkable event; meeting someone from Turkey would have been memorably exotic. The only frame of reference that existed for "foreigners" were the European principalities, the tales of warriors left from the Crusades and the few accounts of adventurers such as Marco Polo.

The American Indians the colonial English encountered were not simply "other" like people from Spain or the Netherlands; they were "primitive" beyond all European experience. The English saw a people who lacked a written language, dwelled principally in temporary structures as nomads, and largely subsisted as hunter-gatherers (though many did practice seasonal farming). Nor, of course, did they have any concept of English common law.

Though much land in the colonies was nominally purchased from local Indian tribes, conflict was inevitable. It was simply not in the consciousness of English colonial leaders to recognize that the natives had any property rights necessary to care about; after all, the Indians themselves did not even recognize ownership of property as the English did. Bit by bit, Indians felt squeezed, pushed, and overwhelmed by the invaders with their amazing technologies. Just as Governor Berkeley crushed the alliance of Indians under Opechancanough in the 1640s, in 1675 New Englanders fought and defeated the Wampanoag Indians and their allies in King Philip's War. Indian wars, skirmishes really, would continue for another century. And, of course, they continued through the 1800s in the wild, then unknown, expanses of the West.

In the Northeast, Abenaki populations had shrunk considerably before the arrival of English colonists.

It wasn't English gunpowder and manpower that did in the Indians, though, but European disease. Through the 1600s, the indigenous Indian population declined by three quarters. Certainly contact with the English brought exposure to viruses for which the native Indians had no immunity; there were recurring smallpox epidemics, for instance. Typhus was prevalent. The principal villain, however, may have been tuberculosis. Recent research now suggests that tuberculosis was the chief culprit in the decimation of Indian population before Europeans arrived on the continent—transmitted possibly by seals. In the Northeast, Abenaki populations had shrunk considerably before the arrival of English colonists.

THE ABENAKI NATION: THE PEOPLE OF THE RISING SUN

The north and northwestern frontiers of the colonies were the domain of the Abenaki Nation. That sounds too grand a term, though, for what was a loose confederation of tribes and subtribes, many of them small. They shared a language (with many local variations), tribal affinities and culture, and a way of life. There was, though, no centralized government between them or necessarily any common cause. Influence and authority lay with individual tribal chieftains and sachems—warriors and wise men.

Ethnologists divide this people into two confederations. The Eastern Abenaki occupied the region of southern Atlantic Canada (New Brunswick and Nova Scotia) and Maine to the Piscataqua River. The Western Abenaki ranged across New Hampshire north to lower Quebec and the St. Lawrence River, as well as northeastern Massachusetts, and west to Lake Champlain. Across this vast northern forest, tribes gathered their villages along the major rivers and principal lakes, often occupied only for part of the year.

Tribes and subtribes came together in villages along the rivers in spring, when the fish such as salmon and shad run upstream to spawn. Falls become fish ladders and fish easy to harvest. Men would fish and hunt through the summer. Women would plant and nurture a "holy trinity" of corn, beans, and squash. The customary planting fashion was to plant beans around a cornstalk, with squash on the outside ring. The cornstalk then becomes a pole for the beans to climb, while the broad leaves of the squash provide ground cover keeping moisture in and nutrient-sucking weeds out.

In the autumn, tribal villages would break up, spreading inland in extended family groups seeking the protection of the forest beside smaller streams for an encampment through the long northern winters. Abenakis lived in substantial, but temporary, housing. Dome-shaped wigwams were built family-sized with frames of bent, flexible saplings interwoven with smaller wands and branches. The infrastructure was then overcovered with birch bark lashed to the frame. Inside, raised sleeping platforms of branches were covered with furs, with storage space for tools and implements beneath. Walls were lined with furs of beaver, fox, bear, and other animal pelts for warmth through the dark, cold months from November through March. In the middle was a central hearth. The fire provided heat and indoor cooking during inclement weather.

The Abenaki left a lasting legacy to their colonial displacers. In early spring when snowmelt came and sap started to rise in the deciduous hardwoods, the Abenaki tapped sugar maples and birch, gathered sap,

To the left of the Abenaki wigwam, work has begun on a dugout canoe. Such white-pine dugouts were sometimes large enough to hold up to forty. Abenaki men used such dugouts on fishing and scouting expeditions, and to carry goods—or warriors.

and boiled it into a sweetening syrup and candy. Throughout northern New England and Quebec today, the annual production of maple syrup is a rite of spring, an economic boon, and a tourist attraction.

The names of tribes and names of rivers or place-names along it are often the same. Eastern Abenaki tribes include the Kennebec, Penobscot, Ossipee, Androscoggin, and Passamaquoddy. Western tribes included the Winnipesaukee, Missiquoi, Pemigewasset, Nashua, and Sokoki. Along the navigable Merrimack River, one of the first waterways to be settled in earliest colonial expansion beyond the coast, the principal tribe was the Pennacook—among the largest and most influential of the western tribes. Their principal village was spread along the broad river valley below Amoskeag Falls, south of present-day Manchester, New Hampshire. Pennacook villages ran southeast along the river toward its estuary in Newburyport.

From the time of Plymouth's settlement to the 1670s, the Pennacook were led by the sachem and chieftain Passaconaway, who repeatedly attempted to reach deals and make peace with the growing English presence. Reputedly a giant of a man, Passaconaway's decades of growing influence and authority came over a tribe that grew weaker and smaller. Among the first tribes with significant European interaction, the Pennacooks were first and worst to suffer from the New World diseases and death tolls that rolled through their villages in waves. Intermittent conflict with neighboring tribes and colonials added further to the tribe's decimation. By the conclusion of King Philip's War in 1678, the Pennacooks and their chieftain scattered north toward Quebec, uniting with other tribes, and their identity largely disappeared. Though history is silent, legends abound concerning the fate of Passaconaway.

The way was now open for colonization along the Merrimack. Conflict with the Abenaki tribes across the region, however, continued. Indian attacks and raids were a constant danger on the frontiers of the gradually westward-pushing colonies right through the mid-1700s. With the European population growing steadily, of course, and the Indian population in constant decline from the ravages of disease, it was indeed a forlorn hope that the steady English advance could be halted.

THE DEFINING GEOGRAPHIC DIVIDE

The great majority of people coming in to New England, the mid-Atlantic colonies, or Virginia were farmers. They knew how to adapt to live off the land and expected to, to build lives and thrive from the soil and animal husbandry. In fact, farming in the South has always been a more profitable venture than in the North. That, too, contributed to the development of our colonies.

Where the dividing line lies between North and South in America has always been a somewhat contested notion. Since the War between the States, we have thought of it in rather artificial terms: the Mason-Dixon Line. As you travel down along the Atlantic coast, the landscape and the seascape change south of New York. The flats of the Jersey Shore jump the mouth of the Delaware River onto the Delmarva Peninsula, and the relatively featureless landscape continues south to the mouth of the Chesapeake. Somewhere along the way, you've entered the South.

In actuality, though, the real division between North and South is more marked farther inland, geographic and quite abrupt. West of the Delaware River Valley, the mountains of eastern Pennsylvania mark the dividing line—the southern border of the glacier advance of the last Ice Age. Eons ago, to the north of the Pennsylvania mountains, advancing glaciers scrubbed the landscape, scraping the topsoil and pushing it before them. When the glaciers slowly retreated, the melt water carried that topsoil grain by grain into the fertile fields of south-central Pennsylvania, the Catoctin Valley, and the broad river plains of the Potomac and the Shenandoah.

The landscape to the north was swept of its rich soil, leaving behind a landscape of exposed rock and fieldstone, craters gouged into the hills and dense evergreen-dominated forest. Perhaps the most dramatic visible distinction is the lakes. From the Poconos north across New York and New England, coldwater, mountain river, and spring-fed lakes riddle the countryside. South of the mountains, lake waters are few and far between and often fed by slow-moving creeks, not glacial springs. In the state of Virginia there are two proper lakes. In the much smaller state of New Hampshire there are more than two hundred, and only two townships that don't include a lake at least partially within their boundaries. The distinction is very visible along the course of Interstate 81 that crosses the eastern mountains of Pennsylvania into central New York. In brief, Scranton is a northern city; Harrisburg is a southern city.

To the south, the landscape was ripe for the economic activity the early settlers expected. Put another way, the land was easy to farm; the fields were easy to till, the soil was rich and fertile, and it might have been hot but the growing season was long. Whether the land was held by the large plantations of the Tidewater and the Piedmont, the small-stake farms won by men who labored off their indentures or the German immigrants beginning to spread out their farms in Lancaster County, the conditions were right for a profitable agricultural economy.

For Virginia through the late 1600s, recognized and promoted by William Berkeley, the "brown gold" of tobacco was an industry far

The Gundalow:
Indispensable for Two Hundred Years

Built in 2011, the seventy-foot gundalow *Piscataqua* carries thousands of students each year and runs public sailings daily through the summer season from its dock on Portsmouth Harbor.

The New World rivers, navigable to their fall lines, were indeed the highways for settlement and commerce from the coastline harbors into the interior of the colonies. "Navigable," however, does not mean that the rivers were accessible to the oceangoing ships that carried passengers and cargo across the Atlantic.

On the tidal estuaries from Maine to the Chesapeake, for two hundred years that job was done by barges often known as gundalows. The idea was hardly new. Barges have carried kings and cargo on the River Thames for a dozen centuries. As with so many aspects of settling the Atlantic coast, English colonists had to adapt to local conditions.

There were many forms of these barges, and many were homemade by farmers and fishermen. They were flat-bottom vessels with a shallow draft enabling them to navigate the tidal rivers. Essentially, gundalows were designed to be powered by the tide, sailing upriver with the flood and returning downriver with its ebb.

The Piscataqua gundalow developed in Portsmouth adapted to serve one of the largest East Coast estuaries—ferrying cargo into the network of seven tidal rivers that drained 930 square miles of watershed. They fed the Piscataqua through brackish Great Bay some fifteen miles inland and encompassing more than two hundred miles of shoreline. What began in the mid-1600s as undecked barges with auxiliary power from long oars or poles, by the turn of the century had become fully decked and powered by a unique short-masted sail called a lateen sail that could be lowered to pass under bridges; it was capable of carrying fifty tons of cargo. It is no coincidence that the vessels resemble the wherries, single-sail barges that have long plied the river network of the Norfolk Broads across northern East Anglia. Many early New England settlers came from the region.

From schooners at Portsmouth Harbor, gundalows carried goods from Europe and the West Indies to towns along both sides of the river system—Dover, Exeter, Durham, and a growing number of others. Downriver, they carried lumber, fish, bricks, and farm produce. Over the years, that cargo increasingly included manufactured goods. It is estimated that more than two thousand gundalows sailed the Piscataqua between 1650 and 1850, with four hundred or more plying the estuary at any given time.

The coming of the railroads rendered the gundalow obsolete in the mid-1800s and they gradually faded from the rivers. The Piscataqua's last commercial gundalow was launched from Durham in 1886.

removed from the subsistence farming of the North. It's the old, old story: Create a market, control the delivery of the product, and you have a commercial winner. Berkeley himself experimented seriously with serioculture—the production of silk—in Tidewater Virginia, but the profitable export crop was tobacco.

As the old saw known by every Yankee farmer goes: The principal crop of New England fields is rocks.

In New England, by contrast, the landscape was not easily adaptable either to dairy farming or grain crops (let alone tobacco or eventually cotton). As the old saw known by every Yankee farmer goes: The principal crop of New England fields is rocks. The classic Currier & Ives / Robert Frost image of New England is those lovely stone walls lining fields and older roads. And true it is. Almost any old road through rural New England bears testimony. Every stone on every wall was dug from the field by hand, with shovel, spade, and crowbar, lifted onto a stoneboat and dragged to the edge of the field. There, stone by stone, it was hand-lifted by two or more men into a weather-eye-determined place on the growing wall.

Before the process of taking out the stones, of course, the land had to be cleared, once again, by hand. Every tree felled, limbed, and removed; every stump dug out or burned; all the brush and groundcover cleared. Then the land was ready to be plowed, by beast-drawn blades turning up or stumbling over the stones that made their way to that wall. Winters were harsh and the season for arable or vegetable crops was the end of May until late September. Spanning that time, the land had to produce enough grain and fodder to winter over livestock from November to early April. Neither the climate nor the land held conditions ripe for an agricultural economy.

Though seventeenth-century colonies were settled and framed by people with very different religious convictions, worldviews, and developing social institutions, it was this geographic divide that may have been the most significant factor in how the colonies and their economies developed through the eighteenth century.

CHAPTER 14

Settled: A Cultural Divide and a Southern Border

It is the true duty of every man to promote the happiness of his fellow creatures to the utmost of his power.

—WILLIAM WILBERFORCE

BY THE EARLY 1700S THE CHARACTER OF THE COLONIES HAD TAKEN shape. There was an indelible and different ethos to the South and to the North, with Pennsylvania's mid-Atlantic sphere of influence both a geographic and political bridge.

THAT NORTH AND SOUTH DIVIDE

The Massachusetts Bay Colony settled by the first Bostonians in 1630 spread over the next few decades into the New England colonies of New Hampshire, Rhode Island, and Connecticut as well as Massachusetts. What was colonized as Virginia spread to include the Carolinas and the southern Delmarva Peninsula. Given what we've already seen of the first establishment of these settlements, the motives of the earliest colonists and the communities they established, it is hardly surprising that the regional societies they spawned and developed were very different—in what are generally overlooked but obvious ways.

Education and attitudes toward education in the early colonies serve as a clear example. To the Puritan New Englanders, general literacy and a keen interest in learning was a by-product of their Reformation worldview—everyone ought to be able to read in order to read the Bible for themselves (and such timeless classics as *Fox's Book of Martyrs* and *The Pilgrim's Progress*). Moreover, education was valued as an adjunct to the responsibilities of citizenship as free men.

Harvard College was already well established, explicitly in order to educate the coming generations of pastors for the Congregational churches of New England. In the process it became a center of classical learning and a natural training ground for teachers. Yale, Princeton (the College of New Jersey), Brown, Columbia, and Dartmouth would follow in the next few decades.

Attitudes to education were very different in royalist Virginia. Governor Berkeley famously said that "I thank God there are no free schools nor printing, and I hope we shall not have these hundred years; for learning has brought disobedience, and heresy, and sects into the world, and printing has divulged them, and libels against the best government. God keep us from both!"

The establishment of the College of William & Mary in Williamsburg in 1693 was expressly for the education of the plantation-owning, governing class's sons. Education was indeed a stepping-stone to advancement, and not something to be trusted to the lower orders. Of the nine colleges and universities that were chartered in our colonial years to 1776, only William & Mary was in the South.

> *I thank God there are no free schools nor printing, and I hope we shall not have these hundred years.*

The cultural differences in the attitude to education established early in the seventeenth-century colonies certainly helped shape the differences in the societies of the North and the South that extended well into the twentieth century and are still in evidence today. It is hardly news to observe that public schools and the expectations and motivation of students are very different in rural New York and New England from their counterparts in the rural South from the Carolinas to Louisiana.

There is a reason why a large percentage of the most selective colleges and universities in the country are within two hundred miles of Boston. On the other hand, the South's "command culture" has throughout our history always turned out superb military leaders. The great majority of our military academies and colleges are there, including such stellar schools as Virginia Military Institute and The Citadel.

To American sensibilities of the twenty-first century it sounds grating on the ear, but New England purposed by religious conviction a society of free and equal individuals, while the Virginia colony believed as strongly in the hierarchical society, that "great chain of being" that they had always known. The colony of Virginia continued to prosper through the last decades of the seventeenth century, and by 1700 had become the most populous and wealthy of the English colonies in the Americas.

From a belief in the God-ordained natural hierarchy of the world and of human society, it was a natural and small step to the institutionalization of race slavery. After all, if everyone is not created equal to begin with, then there must be a basis on which these gradations of status are defined. It was the will of God; the way that reality was ordered.

So those second sons of the English aristocracy famously became the "First Families of Virginia." Their English retinues, retainers, and indentured laborers who made the crossing with them, however, were no better equipped by genes and life experience to the realities of physical labor in the climate of the coastal South than the first Jamestown settlers. The physical demands of the tobacco and later cotton fields were staggeringly unrealistic. On the other hand, the Africans who were enslaved on the West Indies sugar plantations were quite well adapted to the hot, humid climate. Importing them solved both an economic and a rising social problem. Those English indentured servants were working off their indentures and claiming land of their own.

No, the landowning aristocracy of the South did not see a moral problem with race slavery, any more than they saw a moral problem with their indentured bondsmen and tied laborers either in England or in Virginia. The first black Africans brought to Jamestown came on a Dutch ship as indentured servants in 1619. Within a generation, they did not get out of their indenture, and race slavery became hereditary.

PRESSURE TO CONFORM TO THE NORM

In New England, by contrast, society was being molded by the Reformation doctrine of the priesthood of the Believer—and the privacy of that personal priesthood. Salvation was an individual responsibility and a result of personal faith rather than the intercession of the church. New England Congregationalists were fond of recalling Paul's assurance to Timothy in 1 Tim. 2:5: "For there is one God and one mediator between God and man, the man Christ Jesus." An individual's relationship with God was personal, not the business of the church or neighbors or community.

The individualization of faith and the sanctity of an individual's personal relationship with God became a hallmark of New England's Puritan Congregationalists, and of New England society—again, in ways still in evidence today. Over time, it became something of bad form to make personal inquiries into an individual's personal beliefs and convictions. The autonomy of the individual's spiritual and emotional life became characteristic of the old Yankees' social interaction. At the same time, that sense of not being accountable to clergy or social "betters" for one's self or soul was viscerally liberating—still reflected today in the state motto of New Hampshire, famously recorded on its license plate: Live Free or Die. It derives from Gen. John Stark's rallying words at the 1777 Battle of Bennington.

In his essay *Notes on the Definition of Culture*, T. S. Eliot posits astutely that though religion and culture are not synonymous, they are inseparable: Whether nationally or regionally, the dominant religion inevitably finds its reflection in the culture. In the New England orbit, that dominant "religion" is Congregationalism. In the South, the culture reflects the dominance of its Anglican roots—Episcopalian—as well as its particularly "southern" Baptist heritage. Whether or not the members of the society personally subscribe to the tenets and faith of these churches really doesn't alter their local cultural and social patterns. The pervasive cultures that these denominations reflect and created were largely established three hundred years ago.

The Anglican Church that was established in Virginia through the 1600s remained, and largely remains, the church of the leadership class—professionals, "old money," education, and affluence. The Baptist Church

Race Slavery in New England

While the culture and circumstances were quite different in the North, New England was not immune from the taint of African slavery. By the early 1700s, some ships began to return to Boston with a cargo in human bondage. In a few decades there were some fifteen hundred enslaved persons in the colony.

The ethos of the Puritan society, however, was not comfortable with the practice of race slavery, regardless of its legality under English law. In addition, unlike in the agrarian South, the northern economy was not built on industries that made black slavery overarchingly profitable. Though the number of Africans was small overall, there was also a free African society as well in New England, accepted in their communities with general ease.

It was not in the colonies, South or North, however, that any active political voice was raised against the growing slave trade, and that took several generations to germinate. It wasn't until 1787 that a concerted campaign was joined in England by William Wilberforce, MP for Hull, to abolish the British slave trade. Elected an MP for Yorkshire from Kingston-upon-Hull in 1780 when only twenty-one, Wilberforce became the leader of the abolitionist movement and spent almost twenty-five years on his moral crusade. He was present for the vote when the Slave Trade Act was at last passed by Parliament in 1807 and active in the abolitionist cause until his retirement in 1825 after forty-five years in Parliament. The University of Hull is home to the Wilberforce Institute for the Study of Slavery and Emancipation.

This statue of William Wilberforce stands before his birthplace in Hull, the Wilberforce House Museum. Permanent displays unpack the story of the transatlantic slave trade and Wilberforce's campaign for its abolition.

eventually became the church of the underclass to be followed by the Methodists in the later 1700s—the smallholding farmers, the undereducated, and those who labored for others; in other words, for everyone else. Both the episcopate of the Anglicans, however, and the particularly Southern expression of Baptist theology were top-down "command" hierarchies. While the Episcopal Church may have had the bishops that the Puritans eschewed, the Low Church Baptists placed their pastors in that position. What the pastor said, in or out of the pulpit, must be right.

The measure of an individual was not reflected in their wealth or possessions, or even their education.

In New England the dominant Congregational Church reflected the egalitarianism of its Reformation doctrine: We're all in this together. While the first generations of New England colonists carried this to an extreme in their search for "the city on the hill" with a damaging if pragmatic insistence on consensus both in church and civic affairs, the values that equally give every individual a voice remained. The measure of an individual was not reflected in their wealth or possessions, or even their education.

On the other hand, the need to be in public harmony led to a society that earned a reputation for being "cold." Its citizens valued privacy and kept their feelings and judgments to themselves. The best way to maintain harmony with the community was to mind your own business and keep your private opinions to yourself. Civility was the public face. Public behavior was expected to conform. It was repressive and dour by the norms of today's society. Far more assured of their place and identity, wherever it might be in the social hierarchy, Southerners were warmer, open, and hospitable.

The differences in the societies of North and South, which broadly remain to this day, though certainly far less pronounced in the twenty-first century, were clearly defined by 1700. A simple but dramatic illustration lies in the very way towns physically organized, more reflexively than by deliberate town planning, that is still very evident today.

In New England, the center of every market town, geographically and emotionally, was the town meeting house. Sometimes, the town hall shared the central white clapboard building with the Community or Congregational church; sometimes, they were across the street from each other. The town was focused around these emblems of community. In Virginia and its sphere-of-influence colonies to the south, the center of town was the courthouse. Attendant law offices, commerce, and churches radiated from there. The town was focused on the emblem of authority.

But Bridges Were Coming

Through the first decades of the 1700s and the coming of the several King Georges, the ideological and religious hegemony of the oldest colonies—New England and Virginia—was beginning to dissipate. The reasons prompting emigration from Britain had changed with the times. Doors were open for economic and religious migrants from across Western Europe in many colonies actively seeking growth and labor. Trade between the colonies and mutual agreements with neighboring colonies over a variety of interests helped break down barriers as well.

At the same time, the natural boundaries of the English colonies were being reached and challenged. To the north lay New France; to the vague south was Spanish territory and farther west French Louisiana. If the colonies did not see the necessity for creating a united front against both the adversarial powers seeking their own colonial expansion, King George II's ministers certainly did.

Georgia on My Mind

In 1732 King George II issued a charter for the colony of Georgia (conditional on the colony being named after him) to James Oglethorpe, MP. A settled Georgia would provide a buffer between Spanish Florida and the growing Carolinas. To its west lay French Louisiana.

Both a social reformer and philanthropist, Oglethorpe had presented a comprehensive plan that he and several interested friends had drawn up for the settlement of Georgia. They would be the trustees of the new colony. The Oglethorpe Plan provided for limitations on landownership and land grants in fifty-acre parcels to promote family farming, town and village planning, secular self-governance, and religious and social equality. Slavery was prohibited. In short, the last of the thirteen colonies was the most "modern," incorporating Enlightenment ideas that were beginning to course through English salons. Controversially, Oglethorpe's plan intended to settle the colony in part with struggling poor laborers and those languishing in debtors' prison.

The following February, 1733, Oglethorpe and the first 114 settlers aboard the *Anne* landed ashore near what would become Savannah. In a departure from other early colonial settlements, Oglethorpe quickly made friends with Tomochichi, chief of the local Yamacraw Indians, and the settlement grew unhindered. The town they laid out followed a grid pattern around squares, as the Oglethorpe Plan devised. In the ensuing few years, Oglethorpe oversaw the building of a string of defensive forts, and settlement began. In the event, few of Oglethorpe's "worthy poor" and debtors made their way to Georgia. The new colony did, however, attract poorer artisans and laborers as well as Scots and European religious refugees, including a congregation of forty-three Jews from London.

In the War of the Austrian Succession, fought in Georgia as the War of Jenkins' Ear, in 1740 Oglethorpe led a number of successful raids on Spanish forts. An attack by Spanish forces in 1742 saw Oglethorpe organize local militia, defeat and send packing the Spanish at the Battle of Bloody Marsh. The next year, Oglethorpe returned to England and rose through the ranks of the British army. Gen. Oglethorpe never did come back to his Georgia colony, although he lived until 1785. The 1748 Treaty of Aix-la-Chapelle confirmed England's ownership of Georgia.

Despite the careful planning and sound footing upon which Georgia was established by Oglethorpe and his fellow trustees, it was inevitable that their ideal society would become shattered by the slings and arrows of the outrageous real world.

The colony's infrastructure and its port of Savannah grew as the Spanish threat ended. Its land became more inviting. At the same time, economic conditions in England had improved, and migration to the New World became less enticing. The source of indentured labor largely dried up, and labor became in short supply. The province ended its prohibition of slavery in 1749.

Rosewell Plantation: Successful Accomplishment and Conspicuous Wealth

The movement of Virginia's capital to Williamsburg in 1699 spurred English settlement north of the York River to what became Gloucester County. Several of Virginia's "First Families" developed large plantations there early in the eighteenth century. Among them was the Page family. In 1725 Mann Page began construction of Rosewell, on the north bank of the York River near what a century before had been the Powhatan center of Werowocomoco. The mansion was ultimately completed by Page's son, Mann Page II, and remained the family seat for more than a century.

Many historians regard Rosewell as the grandest, most beautiful home constructed in our colonial era. Built of brick, imported mahogany, and marble, Rosewell boasted three floors above a working basement with twelve thousand square feet of living space—twice the size of the newly constructed Governor's Palace in Williamsburg. Sweeping formal gardens opened to views down to the York River.

Unhappily, the mansion of Rosewell was destroyed by fire in 1916. Today, its elegant ruins are maintained by the Rosewell Foundation and open to the public.

Though Rosewell is not difficult to find from Route 17 and Gloucester, expect to drive a dozen miles of rural back road and finally down a dirt track with grass in the middle to park in a field. As remote as the setting is now, there is an eerie romance about the place—perhaps ghosts from its years as one of Virginia's most powerful social settings.

Planters with ready capital from the Carolinas moved down through the 1750s and bought up the agrarian land, pricing the locals out of the market (it's an old, sadly familiar story). To work these new plantations, a steady influx of enslaved Africans made Savannah a bustling, wealthy port. When the charter of Georgia was transitioned from the trustees to a royal colony in 1752–1754, Savannah was designated the colonial capital.

The southern border of the American colonies was now largely a settled matter and relatively secure. Concluding the same on the colonies' western and northern frontiers was another matter.

CHAPTER 15

Setting Up the Great Scots Migration

Nationality is a very curious thing. The blood is Scots and the tempera-
ment is Scots, but I am, in fact, 100 percent American.
— ALEXANDER MACKENDRICK

BY THE TIME GEORGIA WAS CHARTERED AND SETTLED IN 1733, COLONI-
zation of the English coastline of North America was defined. There was
no more empty space to grant, and the principal river estuaries and natural harbors had been spoken for. And it was indeed all *English* coastline.
Since the Acts of Union in 1707, however, the kingdoms of England and
Scotland and their Parliaments had been united. The colonies may have
been English, but that country and the colonies were also now Great
Britain.

In North Britain, as Scotland was often referred to at the time, events
were unfolding that would bring waves of hopeful Scots and Scots-Irish
people to the colonies in search of land and a new home.

THE SCOTS AND SCOTS-IRISH PEOPLE OF THE 1700S

The Plantation of Ulster was the organized colonization of the northeast
province of Ireland. It had began during the reign of King James I. King
James had seen the Plantation to be "a civilizing enterprise" that would
relocate Protestants in Ulster, a land that was mainly Gaelic speaking
and Catholic. Colonizing Ulster with Protestant and English-speaking
settlers was seen as a way to prevent further rebellion and to Anglicize
the Irish.

Scottish colonists were Presbyterian, and the English planters from Cumbria and Northumberland were generally Church of England. Most of the Scottish planters were recruited from the Lowlands and the lawless, unstable Borders. It was certainly hoped that exporting the Border reivers (cattle raiders) to Ulster would help pacify the Borders as well as contribute to British muscle in Gaelic Ireland.

By 1630 there were an estimated eighty thousand British Protestant settlers in Ulster. Through the tumultuous decades of civil war and Commonwealth, the province was subject repeatedly to rebellions and localized conflicts. Then, a famine in Scotland in the 1690s drove another wave of Scottish immigration to Ulster as tens of thousands fled the Border region. By the early eighteenth century, Scottish Presbyterians had become the majority community in the six counties of Ireland's northernmost province.

After King James II fled England in 1688, he looked to Ireland to muster support for a reconquest of his kingdoms. The great majority of Irish were Catholic supporters of a king that promised them greater freedoms and religious liberty. In March 1689 James landed in Kinsale with six thousand French soldiers and marched on Dublin, where he was popularly received. That May King James II held an Irish Parliament in Dublin that reversed property confiscations of the 1650s and confirmed the support of the Irish landed gentry. Then, with a Jacobite army of Catholics, Protestant Royalists, and French, James marched north to join what became the Siege of Derry. British warships arrived and relieved the besieged city that summer.

Having gathered an army of thirty-six thousand soldiers, King William III landed with a fleet of three hundred ships at Carrickfergus on June 14, 1690. Marching south toward Dublin, they met the Jacobite army, which had taken up defensive positions on the south bank of the River Boyne near Drogheda. On July 1st William attacked their position, fording the Boyne at several places and forcing the Jacobites to retreat to avoid being surrounded.

The Battle of the Boyne was not militarily decisive and casualties on both sides were not high—around fifteen hundred Jacobites and five hundred Williamites were killed. However, it proved enough to collapse

James's confidence of victory in Ireland. He rode ahead of his army to Duncannon, and from there returned to France. King James's flight to exile was deemed a desertion by Irish supporters, and the remaining Jacobite army was demoralized and badly hit by desertion as well. They abandoned Dublin and fled west to Limerick. The Williamites marched into Ireland's capital without a fight. The next year, the Jacobite cause ended completely with defeat at the Battle of Aughrim and the surrender of Limerick.

The Williamite victory in Ireland ensured that James II would not regain his throne. It also cemented English dominance over Ireland for centuries. The Protestant ruling class came to be known as the Protestant Ascendency. Both the majority Irish Catholics and the Ulster Scottish Presbyterians were left without political power.

In Ulster, however, King Billy is a hero. The Battle of the Boyne and the Siege of Derry are commemorated as victories for religious liberty and celebrated on July 12. The Troubles in Northern Ireland that blighted two twentieth-century generations found their focal point here.

For more than a century after the war, Irish Catholics maintained a sentimental attachment to the Jacobite cause. At least one composite Irish battalion (five hundred men) fought on the Jacobite side in the uprisings all the way up to the Battle of Culloden in 1746.

That Scottish Presbyterians had heartily supported King William, yet were excluded from power by the postwar Anglican Ascendency, however, was hardly forgotten. Through the eighteenth century, there was a rising resentment of their virtual English overlords, as well as continued conflict with their Catholic Celtic neighbors. The Ulster Scots had also run out of room. The fertile farmland that attracted British settlement in the first place had attracted too many of them and fertilized population growth.

INTO THE VIRGINIA BACKCOUNTRY

In the late 1600s none except the Indians knew the land west of the Blue Ridge. Governor Berkeley hired a German physician and adventurer, John Lederer, to make several expeditions in 1669 and 1670 exploring what became known as the Western Parts or, more commonly, the Backcountry. Lederer ventured over the escarpment of the Blue Ridge Mountains into the accessible and fertile valley of the Shenandoah River.

Beyond the broad river valley to the west lay the sharp accordion ridges of the Appalachians—still largely terra incognita to English colonists in 1700. At that time, it was still widely believed that the Indian Ocean lay tantalizingly close beyond the mountains and the Mississippi.

Governor Alexander Spotswood began encouraging settlement of the frontier valley in 1716, and the first farms and communities emerged over the next decade. Thomas, 6th Lord Fairfax of Cameron, was a teenager in 1719 when he inherited the Northern Neck Proprietary—more than five million acres of Virginia, including the Potomac Valley and the Northern Shenandoah Valley. The value of that land today alone would likely make Lord Fairfax the wealthiest man in the world.

In 1735 he visited Virginia to have his vast holding surveyed, and in 1747 he moved to Virginia to secure and defend his grant. Fairfax encouraged respectable Scots-Irish people, Germans (both Lutherans and the Anabaptist sects), and Quakers to settle and farm the Shenandoah Valley. In 1745 west of the Blue Ridge there were an estimated ten thousand people; five years later, seventeen thousand.

While the Shenandoah Valley was slowly being settled with the rising tide of Scots-Irish and German pioneers moving down the Backcountry, the Appalachian Mountains on the other side of the broad valley proved a natural barrier to westward expansion in the early eighteenth century.

OUT WITH THE STUARTS, IN WITH HANOVER

On King William III's death in 1702, the throne passed to Queen Anne, the Protestant daughter of James II, and Queen Mary's younger sister. She reigned a dozen years, first as Queen of England. In 1707, however, when the Acts of Union formally united her Scottish and English realms, Anne became Queen of Great Britain and Ireland. Alas, though she endured many pregnancies by her husband, Prince George of Denmark, Anne died without a surviving child in 1714.

For almost two hundred years, the island had suffered varying degrees of conflict and contention fueled by religious motivations. The terms of the Restoration had left Parliament clearly "in charge" of the monarchy, and they were not about to risk further religious and social upheaval. By their Act of Settlement 1701, the monarch must be a Protestant.

Most surviving Stuarts in line for the throne were Catholic, and in exile on the Continent. James II had died in 1701 and the heir apparent was his son, James Francis Edward Stuart, who subsequently became known as the Old Pretender. The closest Protestant relative was a minor German prince, George, Elector of Hanover, great grandson of King James I. He was invited to take the British throne, and, as King George I, crossed the channel to his new kingdom at age fifty-four, unable to speak English—and having no desire to learn.

The Stuart legacy had been mixed, to say the least. Most historians rate their dynasty with pretty low marks, over their political ineptness at least. Certainly Britain was optimistic for a change, with the religious turmoil seemingly now behind them. Alas, King George was something of a disappointment. Among other things, he didn't like London, knew nothing of the rest of his kingdom, and didn't much like the people. "German Geordie," as he was scornfully termed, made no secret that he much preferred his comfortable court back in Hanover.

> *Certainly Britain was optimistic for a change, with the religious turmoil seemingly behind them.*

Most English, though, were happy enough to support the new Hanoverian establishment, particularly with the reins of power believed firmly in the hands of Parliament. Not everyone, however, was happy with the settlement—and with the exclusion of the legitimate Stuart heir. In Scotland in particular, Stuart sentiment was strong. After all, this was Scotland's hereditary royal family. That England and the English Parliament would depose their line was felt by many to be a national affront. So, too, English Catholics continued to hold their loyalty to the ousted line of James II. With the Hanoverian ascendency in 1714, those whose allegiance remained with his son, James, "the Old Pretender," became known as Jacobites, as had the Irish supporters of his father.

A Jacobite rising in 1715, often referred to as simply The Fifteen, saw Scottish Stuart loyalists raising their standard in Braemar under the leadership of the Earl of Mar. Over the next few months, Jacobites won control of everything north of the Firth of Forth except Stirling Castle. Though Lord Mar's forces won several small battles, his leadership was generally indecisive and plans for the rebellion rather "seat of the pants."

In November of 1715 an army of Scottish Jacobites moved south into England, drawing some support from English sympathizers, but nowhere near the groundswell of adherents that they had expected. The Hanoverian army caught up with their advance at Preston and in two days of fighting forced the Jacobite surrender. The uprising was over, but not Jacobite dreams.

Ardent Jacobite loyalties lay principally in the Highlands, with the clan chiefs. The allegiances of the Border lairds could be bribed and cajoled. The Lowland earls, however, generally had lands and sometimes titles in England. Their interests lay with the establishment, which was decidedly Hanoverian. Jacobite sympathies simmered and plotted in the Highlands and with an English Catholic minority for a generation.

King George never was comfortable in England, and returned to visit his court in Hanover as often as he could. Besides its familiarity, in Hanover George was an absolute monarch, while in England he had to learn to rule with Parliament. During his reign, the king made half a dozen extended visits to his native Germany, leaving a Regency Council in charge during his absence. It was during these years that Robert Walpole rose as the first among equals of the king's ministers and the office of prime minister evolved. On what became the last of his trips home, King George had a stroke and died in June 1727. He is buried in the chapel at Herrenhausen.

German Geordie was succeeded by his son, the Prince of Wales, George Augustus. George II and his father had never gotten along. Young George had been kicked out of the palace, and his own London home, Leicester House, became a headquarters for his father's political adversaries.

George II made a rather better go at kingship than his father had managed, but the bar wasn't high. The War of the Austrian Succession (1740–1748) largely defined his reign. Fought ostensibly over the succession of Maria Theresa to the Hapsburg throne (the Holy Roman Empire), the war saw Great Britain join in 1743 in alliance with Austria and the Dutch Republic against Prussia and France.

Over here in the colonies, as our tale will pick up, the war was fought out as King George's War. The British captured Louisbourg, the French fortress on Cape Breton Island, Nova Scotia; the French drove English settlement out of the upper Hudson Valley after bloody attacks on Saratoga and Schenectady. Skirmishes ranged across the border with Massachusetts (of which present Maine was a part) with New Hampshire intermittently fighting French Canada to the north.

At the Battle of Dettingen on the banks of Germany's Main River some twenty miles from Frankfort, on June 27, 1743, King George II took command of a thirty-five-thousand-strong allied army of British, Austrian, and Hanoverian soldiers against the French. In the allied victory, George II became the last British monarch to personally lead troops in battle.

The Hanoverian king and most of England's army were in Europe on the front, and fully occupied. Back in Britain, Jacobite sympathizers loyal to the Old Pretender saw opportunity and began machinations to organize another attempt to restore the Stuart throne.

Jacobites and the '45

The Jacobites thought their time had come. The young Stuart heir apparent, Prince Charles Edward Stuart, landed in the Highlands to rally the clans. The Jacobite standard was famously raised at Glenfinnen in August 1745, and the clansmen rallied to the cause: MacDonalds of Clanranald, Camerons, Drummonds and Lovets, Stuarts and Murrays. Bonnie Prince Charlie was bonnie indeed, a handsome, well-spoken youth of twenty-one, capable of securing hearts and allegiance to his father, James's, campaign.

Compared to the ill-fated rebellion in 1715, what became known as the Forty-Five was better led. With Bonnie Prince Charlie as the inspirational figure, the resulting Jacobite army was commanded by Gen. George Gordon Murray, one of the most competent military men of his generation. At the end of the month, the swelling Jacobite force marched south, entering Edinburgh to twenty thousand cheering Scots on September 17th. The next day, King James VIII was proclaimed, with the Bonnie Prince as his regent.

In November, with Prince Charlie at their head, the Jacobites moved south. They won a telling victory at Prestonpans and marched into Cumbria, seizing the cathedral city of Carlisle.

King George II's brother, William Augustus, the Duke of Cumberland, commanded an English army on the Continent. He implored his brother to return him to England with sufficient troops to take on the Jacobite army of rebellion.

Bonnie Prince Charlie and his army made it as far as Derby. Historians assess that if they had pressed, the Stuart force might indeed have taken them to London and perhaps the throne. That's not what happened.

By now, the Hanoverian act was together. Three English armies were converging on the Jacobites, led by Cumberland. The Scots and their allies hesitated. Murray judged they couldn't withstand the redcoats in a pitched battle. Derby was the high-water mark for the Stuart cause. The Jacobite army began a slow retreat back to Scotland, chased by Hanoverian redcoat regiments.

In less than an hour, the dreams of restoring the Stuarts to the British throne disappeared.

After reaching Glasgow at Christmas, Prince Charlie and the Highlanders skirmished through the winter with government forces on a path that led them north through the Great Glen to Inverness. There they were met by the Hanoverian army of the Duke of Cumberland, who marched through the Grampians from Aberdeen to intercept them. The Battle of Culloden on the moors outside of Inverness was quick and decisive.

On April 6, 1746, in less than an hour, the dreams of restoring the Stuarts to the British throne disappeared. The Highlanders made a desperate frontal attack into the disciplined lines of redcoat fire and failed to break the lines. Their disordered retreat was turned into a rout. Some two thousand Jacobite clansmen died in the battle, while Hanoverian casualties numbered a few hundred.

In the battle's aftermath, Cumberland's army pursued the scattering Highland rebels. Bonnie Prince Charlie escaped the battle and fled into the Highlands. After due and sundry adventures, he was smuggled in disguise to the Isle of Benbecula. From there he caught a ship back to

France and never returned to Scotland. A version of the story is told in the haunting ballad "The Skye Boat Song." Flora MacDonald, who facilitated the prince's escape, became a folk hero.

"The Skye Boat Song"'s Romantic Memory

The account of Bonnie Prince Charles Edward Stuart's escape following the Battle of Culloden is best remembered in the popular folk song "The Skye Boat Song." It dates from the late 1800s, however, and isn't an accurate recollection of events. Still, sung to the plaintive tune by which it is known, the song captures Scottish romantic longing and melancholy perfectly. Known around the world by descendents of the Scottish diaspora, it is a favorite of clan societies and a part of the repertoire for bagpipe bands everywhere.

> Speed, bonnie boat, like a bird on the wing,
> Onward! The sailors cry;
> Carry the lad that is born to be King
> Over the sea to Skye.

> Loud the winds howl, loud the rains roar,
> Thunderclaps rend the air;
> Baffled, our foes stand by the shore,
> Follow they will not dare.

The final stanza tells the aftermath of Culloden. It speaks of the desolation and death; but it speaks of undiminished determination and loyal commitment.

> Burned are their homes, exile and death
> Scatter the loyal men,
> Yet ere the sword cool in the sheath
> Charlie will come again.

History had done with the Royal Stuarts, however, and neither the Bonnie Prince nor thousands of Jacobite exiles ever returned to Scotland.

William Augustus, Duke of Cumberland, was hailed a national hero in England. His brother, King George II, and the overwhelming majority of English peers and commoners were grateful that the Jacobite threat was over. Among the monuments and honors Cumberland duly received, the story goes, a flower was named after the duke. Most folks know the variety of dianthus called Sweet William. Up in Scotland, it is sometimes called Stinking Billy.

The Scots Highland clansmen that escaped Culloden and its aftermath were not so fortunate. An Act of Proscription in 1746 disarmed the Highlanders by demanding that their swords be surrendered to the government. It outlawed the wearing of kilts and of the clan tartans. One old McDonald clansman muttered his disgrace, "I ne'er thought I'd be forced ta wear so unmanly a garment as trousers."

Then a series of acts permitting landlords to enclose what had been common land resulted in the forcible displacement of crofters throughout western Scotland in what became known as the Highland Clearances. They were simply kicked out of their homes and off the hill land and valleys they had crofted for centuries. Many of these displaced Highland Jacobites joined the swelling tide of Ulstermen and Lowlanders making their way to North America and a very uncertain new life.

CHAPTER 16

At Home in the Backcountry

"I would rather belong to a poor nation that was free than to a rich nation that had ceased to be in love with liberty."

—WOODROW WILSON

FROM ROUGHLY 1720 THROUGH TO THE 1770S AND THE AMERICAN War of Independence, what began as a trickle became a steady river of emigration. Now thought of as "Scots-Irish," settlers from Ulster, their families and friends from the Borders, and refugee Highlanders from the Jacobite risings became the Fourth Great Migration to the American colonies. It is estimated that 150,000 left Northern Ireland alone for the colonies.

The Ulster Scots, Borderers, and Jacobite clansmen were not simply folks arriving on these shores with a different accent; they were an ethnic group and a distinct people—very unlike New England Puritans, let alone Virginia Royalists or Pennsylvania Quakers. By the early and mid-1700s, however, settlement along the coast from Maine to Georgia had been going on for a century. The Atlantic coast had been well-scouted by now. Prime harbors, anchorages, coves, and coastal plains were the low-hanging fruit that had been taken. The principally agrarian population had spread westward from the coast, taking and making the farmland as it went.

A number of Ulster Scots created New England communities in the 1700s—in what was effectively a northern "backcountry" at the time, if not for long. As early as 1718, Scots-Irish colonists settled Londonderry,

New Hampshire—familiarly naming it for the Ulster town they left behind. In 1720 Scots-Irish farmers made it up the Merrimack River to its natural fall line: Amoskeag Falls. The broad fields of the river valley were ripe for farming, though the falls themselves had been for thousands of years a gathering point in spring and summer for Pennacook Indians who fished the spawning runs of salmon, shad, and lampreys. The Scots settlers named their town Derryfield. (In 1820, after a canal with locks made the Merrimack navigable to the north, the town was renamed Manchester.)

The Scots and Ulster-bred Scots-Irish people weren't terribly welcome, nor were they in a comfortable, familiar society.

This wasn't typical. In truth, in the settled English communities along the Atlantic seaboard, the Scots and Ulster-bred Scots-Irish people weren't terribly welcome, nor were they in a comfortable, familiar society.

As it had been for German Anabaptists and other groups before them, the mid-Atlantic ports were the principal gates of entry for the Scots-Irish migrants. They settled first in Pennsylvania and then across the neck of Maryland and south into western Virginia's Backcountry. Over the coming decades, they moved southwest toward the Great Smokies and down the tangled spines of the Appalachian Mountains. Later in the century Daniel Boone became famous for guiding Scots-Irish settlers through the Cumberland Gap into Kentucky and Tennessee.

The avenue that was available, open, and ultimately led south to the Cumberland Gap and beyond was the Shenandoah Valley. Settlement of Virginia and the plantations that centered its towns and its economy had spread west as far as the first natural barrier to their sprawl: the Blue Ridge Mountains. Running almost three hundred miles north to south along western Virginia, the Blue Ridge is really a long escarpment, a ridge of hills rather than a range of mountains. Nonetheless, its steep, heavily forested slopes would have been a real impediment to travel and transport in the seventeenth century. The other side of the Blue Ridge, the valley of the Shenandoah River spread from the Potomac Valley south to the Tennessee mountains.

West of the Shenandoah, the Appalachian landscape of what is now West Virginia was forbidding: Range after range of steep, thickly forested mountain escarpments running north to south, separated by river valleys of varying breadth and fertility.

Hunters and traders had been exploring the Appalachians from the 1720s; one of their tracks evolved into a primitive road west from Fort Loudoun, now Winchester, Virginia. In 1748 Lord Fairfax began actively encouraging settlement to the west of the Shenandoah, and adventurous settlers began following the track.

During the 1750s that road became an important link west in the French and Indian War. When the war opened in 1754, two forts were built to protect early settlers. At what is now Capon Bridge, Fort Edwards

Among Winchester's earliest settlers was Abraham Hollingsworth, a Quaker who received a land grant of 532 acres in 1734 and built upon it a log cabin. The family became among the most prominent in town. Abraham's son, Isaac, built the present house, the oldest in Winchester, in 1754.

was constructed on the Cacapon River. Farther west, the present-day town of Romney dates its founding in 1754 from the construction of Fort Pearsall, and as such claims status as the oldest town in West Virginia.

From Fort Loudoun west, these small stockades were each a day's march apart for militia heading west to the chain of forts stretching south from Fort Cumberland to Fort Pleasant on Virginia's farthest frontier. A young George Washington traversed this route many times in those years, first as a surveyor and then as a soldier. It was there Washington assumed his first command at age twenty-one.

Today, that early, rough road is part of U.S. Route 50, from Winchester to Parkersburg, West Virginia. The stretch west from Winchester to Grafton is 130 miles. The only town large enough to have a fast-food restaurant along the way is Romney.

To the west of Romney, near Mt. Storm, a roadside historic marker tells a portion of the provisions of the 1763 Treaty of Paris ending the Seven Years' War:

> *By King's Command*
> *The proclamation of George III king of England in 1763 ordered set-tlement west of these mountains to stop. The early treaties between the English and the Six Nations accepted this range as the dividing line between them.*

The king's dealmakers must have scouted the territory well. From that point west, the Appalachian ridges get steeper and the valleys narrower. In fact, between there and Grafton today there are three stretches of Route 50 where prominent signage warns of a 9 percent gradient running for three or four miles—twisting and weaving all the way. That's steep. For a car and driver on well-maintained road, it's a bit of a challenge. When horses drew carts and wagons over a packed-earth track, though, that terrain was a formidable natural barrier to easy migration—or to the movement of militia on foot.

Little by little through the late 1700s and after, however, the constant influx of economic and political migrants from Scotland and Ulster, and their indomitable independence, pushed the frontier farther, bit by bit.

The National Road

Years later, in the 1780s, Washington's experience on that rugged road west over the mountains led him to conceive of an easier route that would become the National Road. It was not finally laid out and constructed, however, until the early 1800s, when it became the most important mid-Atlantic route to the West for decades. Sometimes called the Cumberland Road, it started in Fort Cumberland, Maryland, the limits of navigation on the Potomac. Begun in 1811 and completed in 1837, the first purpose-built, federal highway stretched more than six hundred miles, connecting the Potomac and Ohio Rivers. It followed the general alignment of what is U.S. Route 40 today.

New arrivals over the Appalachian ridges spread south, finding and farming the bottomland in the narrow river valleys.

It was the Anglo-Virginians that moved west of the Blue Ridge, though, who became the small British elite that formed and led communities (many times on land from Lord Fairfax) and established local government. Once again, as it had been in the 1690s after the Battle of the Boyne, the Ulstermen remained subject to an English dominant culture.

At the time of the Revolutionary War, however, population was still thin. (Though no battles in the war were fought in the Shenandoah, loyalists and Quakers who would not be taxed to support American troops were fined or had their property seized.) Before 1775 there were only seven towns in the valley; eighteen more communities were established between then and 1800 as the Shenandoah exploded with settlement in the Great Migration of Scots-Irish people. By 1800 nearly eighty-five thousand people made the valley home.

CULTURE BEYOND THE SEABOARD

On the Scottish Borders not far from the market town of Kelso, Smailholm Tower is one of the best surviving examples of the pele towers that dotted northern England and the Scottish Borders for centuries.

Smailholm Tower belonged to the Scotts; in fact, to the grandfather of Sir Walter Scott, the great romantic novelist of Scotland's history. Visiting there as a boy, the impressionable Scott learned the romances, legends, and ballads that captured his imagination and ultimately his pen.

Pele towers began in the fifteenth century as towers where signal fires could be lit. Subsequently, they evolved into fortified stone-tower houses, generally surrounded by a fieldstone stockade. These pele towers weren't castles, and certainly couldn't survive the onslaught of a full military assault. They could, however, protect an extended family and its dependents and livestock against the depredations of reivers and clan enemies. They were personal defense in a time of lawlessness.

Lawlessness. It's difficult for us to fathom a society without the effective rule of law. Until the late eighteenth century, however, the vast, sparsely populated region of England's northern counties (today the counties of Durham, Cumbria, and Northumbria) and the broad rural Scottish Lowlands south of the Edinburgh/Glasgow line were in practice fundamentally without law.

It would have been their collective instinct to separate themselves from the restrictive expectations of the confidently superior English colonists.

Theirs was a culture without the social restraints and community allegiances that we take for granted. In the absence of any broad restraining loyalty, an effective judiciary, and the powers we take for granted and rely upon in modern law enforcement, a rough Border justice evolved. Primary loyalties were to the extended family and the Lowland clan chiefs. Blood feuds were common, retribution and revenge cycles continued for generations, and violence was the primary means of sorting out differences.

The rugged independence and decidedly rural culture went with the North British to Ulster, and ultimately to the New World. Yes, the Scots-Irish migrants found the coastline already settled with English communities and made their way to the Backcountry and down the Shenandoah and Appalachian valleys. In actuality, though, it would have been their collective instinct to separate themselves from the restrictive expectations of the confidently superior English colonists.

After all, the Scots-Irish people of Ulster, the wild clannish Borderers, or the Highland refugees of the Jacobite risings and the Clearances had no history that led them to easily integrate into an English society, nor had they any reason to embrace its culture or its churches. This was again a time well before the American notion of social equality; the Scots-Irish people would have appeared rustic to their English neighbors and (with all due Christian charity, of course) made to feel it.

Escaping the governance of an elite with an unfamiliar culture may be the iconic paradigm of American identity and the uniquely American ethos—our national subconscious.

In Mark Twain's masterpiece, *Huckleberry Finn*, the eponymous hero personifies that identity. As the narrative events of the novel draw to a close, the reader is left with Huck's conclusion: "But I reckon I've got to light out for the territory ahead of the rest, because Aunt Polly wants to adopt me and sivilize me, and I can't stand it. I been there before."

And so they escaped. The largely Celtic folk from North Britain and Northern Ireland became the first to light out for the territory ahead of "civilization," to follow what became the American narrative from sea to shining sea, to "Go West" many decades before Horace Greeley tossed down his famous gauntlet in 1879. In the late 1700s, "West" was Kentucky, Tennessee, and the mountain ranges beyond the Shenandoah Valley.

The Scots-Irish migrants brought a culture with them into Appalachia and the country beyond the seaboard from West Virginia to Georgia and spreading west. It is still recognizable today, for instance, in the fiddle of bluegrass music, horse racing, and a fondness for weapons. Resilient, independent, and staunchly loyal, with strong family ties and values, these are proud, self-confident country people that love NASCAR, guns, and church.

The Scots brought with them a fondness for whisky, as well. Alas, they had known how to make it for centuries, but the southern climate

The Wilderness Road down the Great Valley

Movement from the coast inland and south through the Shenandoah Valley as well as over the western mountain ridges soon followed a route that became known as the Wilderness Road. It grew through the eighteenth century as settlers spread the frontiers in both directions. Individuals seeking their fortune, couples and families traveling on foot, horseback, and wagon, carrying their chattels, tools, seed corn, and all their worldly possessions followed their dreams.

The road led west from Philadelphia following roughly what is now known as the Main Line (Route 30), through Lancaster and York. At Chambersburg, it turned south crossing the narrow neck of Maryland via Hagerstown, then Martinsburg, West Virginia, to Winchester. Paralleling the Blue Ridge escarpment down the valley to Roanoke, it was known as the Great Valley Road. Along the road, the towns of Middletown, Harrisonburg, and Staunton grew up. You can follow the route of the Great Valley Road today on Route 11, now the ghost road running parallel to Interstate 81 down the Shenandoah.

From Roanoke, the Wilderness Road was wilderness indeed, veering west through Radford to Bristol at what there became the state border with Tennessee. In 1775 Daniel Boone blazed the trail west across the western Appalachians at the Cumberland Gap near Middlesboro on the Tennessee-Kentucky line. In one condition or another, however, the road continued south into North Carolina by the middle of the century.

was not conducive to growing barley. Resourcefully, they made distilling mash from the grain they could grow, corn. And bourbon was born.

The characteristics of a popular culture, social organization, and even language stereotyped in the story of Sergeant Alvin York, *The Dukes of Hazzard* and the famous Hatfield-McCoy feud, and caricatured in *The Beverly Hillbillies*, all came from a people that brought their Celtic folkways with them. When they settled their communities, there was no other indigenous culture with which to blend. They had to adapt to the land and climate, but otherwise did not have to change their way of life for generations.

Inevitably, Scots and Ulster Scots stock spread through the country. Their descendents are those that throng to Scottish Highland Games from Loon Mountain, New Hampshire, to Stone Mountain, Georgia, and belong to clan societies and proudly wear the tartan. They have also contributed more than their fair share of American presidents, from Andrew Jackson to Woodrow Wilson. In fact, however, our uniquely American identity and American culture would be unrecognizable today without the influence and folk culture of this fourth great nineteenth-century migration—just as the colonies were coming of age, and the country becoming ready to be born.

CHAPTER 17

The Wars for North America

*If I were an American, as I am an Englishman, while a foreign troop
was landed in my country, I never would lay down my arms never
never never!*

—WILLIAM PITT

WE DO NOT THINK OF FRANCE AS BEING AN ENEMY IN OUR AMERICAN
colonial past. We remember Lafayette and the invaluable support of the
French in our War of Independence, and think of France in the 1770s
and 1780s as an ally and a national friend. It was not, however, because
France admired, respected, and shared our stated ideas and intentions for
government. The French Revolution and uprising of the people against
their oppressive aristocracy would not come until the 1790s.

In fact Britain had been actively fighting the French in North America and on the Continent for the better part of a century. And these colonies were British and the people thought of themselves as such; Britain's
wars were ours and the colonies' wars were theirs. The French had been
slowly but steadily immigrating into and building the province of New
France around the Gulf of St. Lawrence and inland along the St. Lawrence River to Montreal and beyond for as long as the English colonials
had been settling in North America. They had territorial ambitions to
expand to the west and southward, pushing the vague northern borders
of British possession.

More successfully than the English colonials, the French had built
alliances with Indian tribes forged by trade, bribe, and diplomacy that

provided them with a shifting but effectual combat force as well. Hostilities between the French with their Indian allies and the English colonies were an omnipresent feature of life on the northern colonial frontiers—as they were on the European continent between France and England.

KING GEORGE'S WAR: JUST THE PRELUDE

The stage for the Seven Years' War in North America was set a decade earlier with a conflict fought here as a theater of the War of the Austrian Succession. In the provinces, it was King George's War, between the English colonies and New France and their Indian allies. This was the war that saw King George II lead his army in battle. It was not the first time that the British and French borders in North America came to arms, nor would it be the last.

THE SIEGE OF LOUISBOURG

At the easternmost landfall on Cape Breton Island, itself the eastern land arm of the Gulf of St. Lawrence, the French erected Louisbourg over a period of thirty years, 1710–1740. The fortress complex was the largest, most elaborate defensive fortification built in colonial North America. Its harbor served as a base for French naval control of the St. Lawrence estuary and fishing along the north Atlantic banks, as well as providing a haven for French privateers and a supply depot for goods coming to the province. It was a crucial link between Quebec and France, and a considerable military asset.

When war was declared in 1744 between France and Britain, the French from their base fortress at Louisbourg launched an unsuccessful series of attacks on Fort Anne at Britain's then Nova Scotia provincial capital of Annapolis Royal. That winter a colonial force was organized by the governors of Massachusetts and New Hampshire with support from all the New England colonies, New York, and New Jersey. A flotilla of more than four thousand militiamen on ninety ships sailed from Boston in March 1745. They were met off Nova Scotia by a fleet of English warships in support. The siege of Louisbourg began with a British naval blockade against any relief supplies or reinforcements arriving for the fortress.

Over the next two months, the attacking British colonial army raided, attacked, and subdued the small villages near Louisbourg, and tightened an artillery noose around the French fort. After more than six weeks of siege and bombardment, the French garrison surrendered on June 28, 1745. The commander of the expedition, William Pepperell, was awarded with a baronetcy and a promotion to colonel. Massachusetts's Governor William Shirley was made a colonel as well.

Louisbourg was a big prize for the British, but it hardly put an end to the war. That summer, Abenaki tribes of the Wabenaki Confederation raided British villages all along the Bay of Fundy coast and along the porous Massachusetts border. That November a French and Indian attack leveled Saratoga, New York, and caused the British to abandon all their Hudson River Valley settlements above Albany.

In the long run, the seizure of Louisbourg, as grand an achievement as it was for colonial militia, accomplished nothing. The War of the Austrian Succession proved an inconclusive draw. At the Treaty of Aix-la-Chapelle in 1748, Louisbourg was returned to the French, and the colonial borders of the New World provinces remained as they were before the war. Nothing had been diminished in the adversarial heat between France and Britain—either here in North America or in Europe. The flames of war broke out again in just a few short years.

The intermittent conflict with New France and their Abenaki allies occupied the northern colonies through much of the early and mid-1700s. That was not, however, the only sphere of influence by which the French threatened British colonial interest. The Great Migration of Scots and Ulster Scots-Irish people also helped set the stage for the French and Indian War as they spread to the west in both Pennsylvania and Virginia. At the confluence of the Allegheny and Monongahela Rivers, the French cut them off at the pass at Fort Duquesne, the site of present-day Pittsburgh. That was on the water route that led from the St. Lawrence into the Ohio River Valley and ultimately to the Mississippi. It was central to controlling trade and settlement into the Ohio River Valley and of strategic importance. Here would come the flashpoint of war between France and Britain and their respective allies once again.

FRENCH, INDIANS, AND THE SEVEN YEARS' WAR

While it is known in America as the French and Indian War, on the world stage the conflict was just the North American theater in a broader conflict (that it helped spark) between Britain and France known as the Seven Years' War.

To the extent that Americans learn about this conflict in school, it is generally regarded to be a minor regional war that ended with the French losing. Besides, there are more exciting things coming shortly after in the American colonial rebellion. This war, however, cannot be dismissed as another series of skirmishes that made up the various Indian Wars in the early decades of the colonies.

Involving all of the European imperial powers, the Seven Years' War (1754–1763) was fought across Europe and in North America, Africa, and Asia. It mobilized armies and involved both colonial settlers and indigenous peoples in an unprecedented way. Winston Churchill referred to this conflict as "the First World War." This was a "real" war against a European power where the fighting lasted for years. For France, Spain, and Britain, its outcome determined the fate, geographic divisions, and political makeup of North America.

This was a "real" war against a European power where the fighting lasted for years. Its outcome determined the fate, geographic divisions, and political makeup of North America.

It is something of an irony that what we call the French and Indian War created the proximate cause of the American Revolution—and also resulted in a necessary condition for the colonies' eventual success. When in the course of human events the time came in 1776 for the colonies to take on Great Britain in organized military revolt, what they certainly needed were experienced military leaders. This war provided them.

General Folsom Earns His Rank

In New Hampshire, Exeter's Winter Street Cemetery holds twenty-two graves of Revolutionary War veterans, including Maj. Gen. Nathaniel Folsom (1726–1790). Beside Folsom's grave lies his wife, Dorothy, whose gravestone identifies her as "wife of Col. Nathaniel Folsom." To her right, lies their son, Arthur, who died aged nine, "son of Major Nathaniel Folsom." The general earned his rank beginning as a captain in the New Hampshire Provincial Regiment fighting in the French and Indian War, of course. His wife and son died as he rose through the ranks. Folsom went on to become a delegate to the Continental Congress and was appointed by them to be senior officer of the New Hampshire militia during the Revolutionary War.

Nathaniel Folsom was one of those making up the officer corps of the Continental Army in the War of Independence who had gained their military experience in the Seven Years' War.

By the middle of the 1700s, French interests in North America had spread inland via the St. Lawrence River, embracing Cape Breton and the Bay of Fundy coast known as Acadia, as well as Quebec and Montreal. Via the inland waterway, French traders and trappers extended the influence of New France across the Great Lakes and through the Ohio Valley toward the Mississippi River. In the process, they developed connections and trading partnerships with tribes of Algonquians and the Iroquois Confederation (in addition to their Abenaki allies to the east).

At the same time, English, Scottish, and German settlers were pushing farther west and south in Pennsylvania and Virginia. Their old colonial charters extended the colonies' territorial claims into what at the time they were issued had been still the Great Unknown continent. These contested claims to land and the vital rivers beyond the Appalachians resulted in a series of provocations that could only escalate. Then, the French occupied Fort Duquesne in force.

In 1753 the Virginia governor, Robert Dinwiddie, sent a regiment of Virginia militia west to warn the French off what was claimed as Virginia territory. The officer in charge was Major George Washington, then aged twenty-one. France demurred and sent additional forces into the area.

On a second and stronger expedition the next year, at what became known as the Battle of Jumonville Glen, Washington surprised a French scouting party and inflicted many casualties that included the commanding officer. Instead of pressing forward toward Fort Duquesne and an overwhelming French force, Washington withdrew several miles and built a defensible position—Fort Necessity. The French attacked on July 3, and Washington was compelled to surrender and withdraw. It took weeks for word of these battles to reach London and Paris, but the war had begun.

At the time hostilities began, neither France nor Britain had much of a regular military presence on the continent. That was about to change.

The principal theaters of the conflict in North America were the contested western frontiers—in New York, western New England, Virginia, and western Pennsylvania to the Ohio River Valley, the Champlain Valley and the Canadian Atlantic coast (in particular Nova Scotia and the

St. Lawrence estuary). At the time hostilities began, neither France nor Britain had much of a regular military presence on the continent. That was about to change.

In 1755 London dispatched Gen. Edward Braddock to Virginia to lead an expedition to remove the French. That June Braddock took a command of fifteen hundred British troops and colonial militia with Washington as aide west to take Fort Duquesne. They never made it that far. French and Indian fighters ambushed the column repeatedly and harassed its forced retreat. British losses were heavy, and Braddock himself was mortally wounded in one such raid. Washington led five hundred surviving troops on a withdrawal back to Virginia.

That same summer, the Battle of Lake George ended a northern advance of colonial militia to break French supply lines into the west. The French dug in and built a stockade that became Fort Ticonderoga.

Farther east that year, the British had better success. Just a few years earlier, the French had constructed Fort Beausejour at the head of the Bay of Fundy on the isthmus separating present-day New Brunswick and Nova Scotia. Beausejour was designed to protect the land route, and supply line, between Quebec and Louisbourg. Peninsular Nova Scotia was British territory; New Brunswick and Cape Breton Island were part of New France. In June the fort was taken by a force of British regulars and New England militia led by Col. Robert Monckton.

In addition to isolating the fortress and French supply depot of Louisbourg on Cape Breton's coast, the capture of Fort Beausejour, which the British renamed Fort Cumberland, led to the (sometimes forcible) expulsion of the French settlers along the Bay of Fundy coast—Acadia. This story was told in Henry Wadsworth Longfellow's now little-read narrative poem *Evangeline*, but to this day the coastline from Yarmouth through Digby to Wolfville is still heard referred to as Evangelineland. The displaced Acadians ended up settling in southern French territory—Louisiana. Gradually Acadian became Cajun.

The death of Gen. Braddock brought the appointment of Lord Loudoun as British commander. The years of 1756/57 saw the British flounder to get organized, however, and French and Indian forces took advantage, harassing and raiding the British at Fort Bull and Fort William Henry from Fort Carillon. In May 1756, England formally declared war on France and broadened the conflict to Europe. Britain didn't have much early success there either. The Duke of Newcastle fell as leader of the Commons in 1757, and William Pitt succeeded him in a coalition—with Pitt assuming direction of the British military.

GEORGE WASHINGTON TAKES COMMAND

George Washington was only twenty-three when he presided over the burial of Gen. Braddock in July 1755 and assumed command of the militia and British troops on the retreat from the ill-fated attempt to take Fort Duquesne. One result was that Washington was promoted by Governor Dinwiddie to colonel and "Commander in Chief" of the Virginia colonial militia, responsible for defending three hundred miles of Virginia frontier.

From a well-connected family of Virginia planters, Washington's great grandfather, John, had arrived in the colony in 1656 from the family's

Among the oldest buildings in Winchester, local legend says that a young George Washington used this as an office while on his surveying mission from 1749 to 1752. He returned to it as a headquarters during the building of Fort Loudoun.

ancestral home of Sulgrave Manor in Northamptonshire. After several generations in Virginia, the family had accumulated considerable wealth and property. Very practically, Washington's education had included land surveying at William & Mary. It was in this capacity that Washington had first traveled the Backcountry, began acquiring land in the Shenandoah Valley, and traveled the track over the western mountains to the Ohio River.

In the autumn of 1755 Washington arrived in Winchester and set up office in a log-and-stone building that he had used several years previously as a surveying office. Here, he oversaw the construction of Fort Loudoun—designed to be a staging base for troops moving into the western mountains and south along the valley, as well as his regimental headquarters. Washington moved into the fort upon its completion in December 1756.

In command of a thousand soldiers (the first full-time militia in the colonies), Col. Washington led his regiment successfully in twenty battles over the next year.

His military reputation would not be forgotten; Washington had earned his spurs—and his future command.

The situation in North America changed dramatically in 1758. There had been a poor harvest in New France, smallpox spread through their Indian allies to the west, and the impact of a British naval blockade at the mouth of the St. Lawrence took its toll on both French colonists and soldiers and their commander, Gen. Louis-Joseph, the Marquis de Montcalm.

In the face of a force of six thousand British troops led by Gen. John Forbes, the French withdrew from Fort Duquesne, in effect surrendering control of the Ohio River Valley to the British. After the British had achieved that seminal strategic victory, George Washington retired from his commission in December 1758. Shortly thereafter, he married Martha Custis; they moved to Mount Vernon, where he took up life

Words of Wise Washington

"The foundation of our national policy will be laid in the pure and immutable principles of private morality, and the preeminence of free government be exemplified by all the attributes which can win the affections of its citizens and command the respect of the world."

"Few men have the virtue to withstand the highest bidder."

"To be prepared for war is one of the most effective means of preserving peace."

"Let us with caution indulge the supposition that morality can be maintained without religion. Reason and experience both forbid us to expect that national morality can prevail in exclusion of religious principle."

"It is better to offer no excuse than a bad one."

"Nothing can be more hurtful to the service than the neglect of discipline, for that discipline, more than numbers, gives one army the superiority over another."

"Experience teaches us that it is much easier to prevent an enemy from posting themselves than it is to dislodge them after they have got possession."

as a planter and respected leader in the colony. His military reputation would not be forgotten; Washington had earned his spurs—and his future command.

CHAPTER 18

The Northern Campaign against New France

Canadians understand that immigration, that people fleeing for their lives, that people wanting to build a better life for themselves and their kids is what created Canada; it's what created North America.
—JUSTIN TRUDEAU

WHILE THE VIRGINIA FRONTIER WAS SECURED AND FRENCH EXPANSIONism in the west was being effectively curtailed by Gen. Forbes and Col. Washington, the war did not go so easily in its northern theater and the New France heartland.

A TALE OF TWO FORTS

It is difficult to imagine that as late as the mid-1700s the northern and northwestern frontiers of British colonial North America would neither be clearly defined or secured. Upper New York from the Champlain Valley to Lake Ontario, across the rolling Green Mountains separating Champlain and the upper Hudson River Valley from the Connecticut River and New Hampshire's lakes and White Mountains, and northeast along six hundred miles of forested border merging the province of Maine with Quebec and New Brunswick: This was all vague, contested, and very sparsely populated territory.

In 1735 the Massachusetts General Court chartered four "plantations" for settlement in the Upper Valley of the Connecticut River. Then part of Massachusetts, the four townships on the eastern side of the river were realigned with New Hampshire in a border settlement in 1753: the present towns of Chesterfield, Westmoreland, Walpole, and Charlestown; the northernmost of these was "No. 4." The plantation was settled in 1740 when three Farnsworth brothers moved north up the Connecticut to clear land and farm the broad, fertile river valley. Over the next several years, they were joined by some dozen families farming around a loose settlement spread across half a mile.

No. 4 was the most northwestern settlement in New England. This was the frontier.

In 1743 they literally moved their homes together to build a rectangle of houses around a common square, surrounded by a wooden stockade and guard tower. This was the Fort at No. 4. Some thirty miles upriver from the nearest neighboring settlement at Fort Drummer (present-day Brattleboro, Vermont), No. 4 was the most northwestern settlement in New England. This was the frontier.

The next year, French and Abenaki Indian raiders burned the settlement's outlying farms. Several settlers were killed in Abenaki ambushes and several others were kidnapped back to Canada for ransom—in the term of the day, they were "captivated."

In 1747 Captain Phineas Stevens arrived at No. 4 with a troop of thirty militia. Eleven days later, the fort was unsuccessfully attacked by a force of some three to five hundred French militia and Abenaki warriors under a French officer. They lifted the siege and withdrew back to Quebec after three days.

The town was subject to repeated raids, skirmishes, and captivities over the next few years before the Seven Years' War made official a French and Indian War they had been fighting for a decade already. The most famous of these "captivities" was Susanna Willard Johnson, kidnapped with her family in a 1754 Abenaki raid. After several years in captivity, Johnson was released and wrote a narrative of her story.

The guard tower and main gate of the Fort at No. 4 look quite similar to the late nineteenth-century depiction of cavalry forts across the plains and Wild West. The frontier kept moving to the west after 1760.

During the war years, a number of New England provincial units garrisoned the fort or passed through on their way to fighting in the Champlain Valley or Quebec. Among them, Maj. Robert Rogers and his Rangers put in here on their return from an unfortunately failed raid in Quebec.

In 1759 construction was begun on a seventy-eight-mile road over the rolling Green Mountains that would connect the Fort at No. 4 with the shores of Lake Champlain at Crown Point. Construction of the project was led by Capt. John Stark, who served with Rogers, and accomplished by Stark's company of Rangers and the New Hampshire Provincial Militia under Col. John Goffe. The Crown Point Military Road was intended to carry soldiers and their supplies to forts in the west (the same purpose as the road Washington had helped lay out west from Fort Loudoun).

When the fighting of active war ended with the surrender of Quebec late in 1760, however, the military usefulness of the road ceased as well.

Robert Rogers and His Rangers

The mountainous terrain and densely forested wilderness of North America was unknown and ill-suited to the tactics of the British redcoat regiments sent to fight here. They relied upon units of colonial soldiers who knew the land and the enemy to serve as skirmishers and scouts. Men were recruited from local militias and communities to join these ranger units ("to range the woods"). They were guerilla fighters. The most effective and well known of these units was Rogers' Rangers.

From the southern New Hampshire frontier that had known generations of Indian raids and fighting, Robert Rogers was originally commissioned in 1755 to form a company of sixty-five men as part of the colony's provincial regiment. Rogers and his command proved so valuable in the crucial upper Hudson River Valley that the Rangers were soon attached to the British army as an independent unit. By 1757 Rogers's commission had grown to ten companies numbering more than a thousand men, including formerly enslaved presons and Indians.

Now Major Rogers explained his orders clearly: "From time to time, to use my best endeavors to distress the French and their allies by sacking, burning and destroying their houses, barns, barracks, canoes, boats, etc., and by killing their cattle of every kind; and at all times to endeavor to way-lay, attack and destroy their convoys of provisions by land and water, in any part of the country where I could find them."

In addition to countless raids and skirmishes, Rogers' Rangers took part in the Battle of Ticonderoga, the crucial Siege of Louisbourg, and the Battle of Quebec. After fighting in the North American theater ended, Rogers' Rangers was disbanded in 1761. Among Rogers's lieutenants was Capt. John Stark, who more than a decade later famously became the general commanding colonial victories at the Battle of Bunker Hill and Battle of Bennington.

Having served beside the British officer corps, after the Seven Years' War Rogers spent a number of years in England. When the War of Independence came, he offered his services to the Continental Army, but Washington did not take him on, suspicious of his loyalties. Perhaps just wanting to get into the action, Rogers did change sides and raised a regiment of King's Rangers. The unit proved ineffectual in the colonies, however; Rogers' time as a guerilla leader had long passed its sell-by date. His one notorious act of war was to turn in the colonial patriot Nathan Hale, who was hung as a spy with the famous words: "I regret that I have but one life to give for my country." Almost needless to say, historians and aficionados of the period express very mixed words about the character, skills, and person of Major Robert Rogers.

The only route across what became the state of Vermont—a territory of previously unsettled Indian land—became the highway for settlement in the years following the cessation of the Seven Years' War. The broader plains of bottomland lining the river valleys in the gentler, less rocky Green Mountains made prime land for farming and quickly attracted pioneers.

The end of hostilities with the Abenaki, who largely moved north to Quebec with their French allies, meant that the Fort at No. 4 ceased needing to be a fort as well. In 1753 it formally became Charlestown, named after Admiral Charles Knowles, who had acknowledged Captain Stevens for his service in the fort's 1747 siege.

In 1777, during the Revolutionary War, then Gen. John Stark returned to Charlestown as a mustering point and staging area for his New Hampshire troops, leading to the Battle of Bennington. But the Fort at No. 4 was already a disassembled relic after its years as the frontier.

Meanwhile, in the Champlain Valley

Lake Champlain flows northward 125 miles to the Richelieu River, from whence it joins the St. Lawrence River—the seaway to Montreal, Quebec, and the open Gulf of St. Lawrence. It was the central link in a network of waterways that ultimately connected the Hudson River and New York with New France and Quebec City. Whoever controlled the waterway controlled the land.

From Lake Champlain the primary route south was to portage across a four-mile land bridge to Lake George at a point about twenty-five miles from Champlain's southern end. After sailing Lake George's thirty-two-mile length, there was another portage of a dozen miles south to the Hudson River at Fort Edward. The overland portage path from Lake Champlain was just south of a narrows in the lake with a promontory on its western shore. It was the route's Achilles' heel and a location of strategic military importance. The peninsula was called Ticonderoga—Iroquois for "place between two waters."

After a French defeat on Lake George, above Champlain at the lake's narrows, in 1754 Michel Chartier de Lotbinière began a fortification that was named Fort Carillon. This was not a fortified village with a wooden stockade like the Fort at No. 4, but a purpose-built, state-of-the-art eighteenth-century military base. From its completion the next year, Fort Carillon was the strongest and most strategically located military fortification and base in the chain between the Hudson River and New France.

In 1757 Fort Carillon became the staging area for a massed army of French regiments, provincial militia, and some eighteen hundred to two thousand Indians recruited from various tribes as far west as the Great Lakes under Gen. Louis-Joseph de Montcalm. The force of roughly eight thousand warriors proceeded south across the portage to Lake George. Their objective was an attack on Fort William Henry on its southern shore. Built in 1755, Fort William Henry was an earthwork and log fort, with wooden buildings within its walls. The French and Indian army laid siege to the fort and garrison of twenty-five hundred British regulars and colonial militia on August 5th. After three days of artillery bombardment at increasingly short range, the fort was substantively breached and destroyed, casualties to the garrison troops were high, and the British raised a white flag of surrender.

Under the terms of surrender negotiated by Gen. Montcalm and the British commander, Lt. Col. George Munro, the British and colonial soldiers and camp civilians were to be safely escorted by French soldiers south to Fort Edward—allowed to keep their arms, but stripped of ammunition.

The column formed to move south the next morning, while a disparate and multilingual army of bellicose Indian mercenary warriors swarmed about, thought to be angered because they received no "spoils of war." As the column set out for Fort Edward, unled and undisciplined Indians sacked the fort, killing all the sick and wounded left behind. They attacked the column from the sides and rear, stripping soldiers of their weapons and clothing, killing and scalping at will. The French officers were powerless, and in some cases unwilling, to control or prevent the brutal onslaught brought by their allies. Several hundred British were killed, wounded, or taken captive in the massacre.

The story of the siege, engagement, surrender, and aftermath is told by James Fenimore Cooper in *The Last of the Mohicans*, the second of the early American novelist's *Leatherstocking Tales* of the French and Indian wars and the colonial frontiers—far more widely read a few generations ago than they are today.

BATTLE OF FORT CARILLON

After a disastrous year in the North American theater of war for the British in 1757, plans for the 1758 campaign under the overseeing eye of Secretary of State William Pitt called for three objectives: to take Fort Duquesne, cutting off the French in the west; to take the seemingly impregnable fortress of Louisbourg on the northeastern coast of Cape Breton Island; and to launch an attack on New France through the Champlain Valley. The latter job meant taking Fort Carillon.

The task of massing an assault on the French stronghold fell to Gen. James Abercrombie. Near the charred and tangled remnants of Fort William Henry, the British and colonial army assembled, with regiments of redcoat regulars from England, Scotland, and Northern Ireland and provincial militia from New York, New Jersey, Rhode Island, Massachusetts, and Connecticut, and Rogers' Rangers. Gen. Abercrombie led north an allied army of sixteen thousand on July 5, 1758.

Knowing of British intentions and the strength of their mobilization, Gen. Montcalm arrived at Fort Carillon on the last day of June, finding an undermanned garrison of thirty-five hundred. After the results of several days of surveillance and delaying skirmishes, Montcalm determined to take the fight outside the fort to defend the only feasible approaches on its weaker land-facing north side. In two days, on July 6 and 7, the French constructed earthwork defenses and entrenchments more than a half mile northwest of the fort.

By July 8th, the British force had assembled and battle lines formed. Gen. Abercrombie's intelligence had led him to greatly underestimate the strength of the French defenses. He rashly decided on a strategy of frontal assault without any artillery support. While the log and earthen ramparts of the French lines would have been devastated by cannon, they were an effective defense against small-arms fire.

The Battle of Fort Carillon began in fits and starts. It ended in disaster for the allied British. Scholars of the event are generally agreed that Abercrombie directed an epic failure. He sent three frontal attacks into a killing field of entrenched fire supported by cannon in redoubts at their flanks. During the battle, cannon from the fort sank two barges carrying British artillery and scattering the rest. After three hours of failed fighting along the French line, Abercrombie finally ordered a general and disorganized retreat down to Champlain's shores and back along the portage road to Lake George. British allied casualties numbered nearly twenty-five hundred killed and wounded; the French suffered six hundred casualties and losses. It was the bloodiest battle of the Seven Years' War in North America—and a decisive French victory.

Despite repulsing the British attempted attack on Canada at Fort Carillon, the French were not so fortunate elsewhere in 1758. Fort Duquesne was taken that year without a fight in the face of Gen. John Forbes and his force of six thousand, and Gen. Jeffrey Amherst directed a successful siege leading to the capture of Louisbourg.

In British campaign planning for 1759, Pitt called for Gen. Amherst to undertake the mission Gen. Abercrombie failed at the previous

Three tiers of cannon form the battlements of Fort Ticonderoga looking over the southern end of Lake Champlain. To the right, just past the hill called Mount Defiance, lies the beginning of the portage path to Lake George.

summer: to lead an army up the Champlain Valley to attack Quebec. The other campaign of the summer was to send Gen. James Wolfe, who had distinguished himself at Louisbourg under Amherst, against Quebec City. In late July Amherst led a force of eleven thousand from the south up Lake George and against Fort Carillon, holding then a meager garrison of four hundred French soldiers. The British began to entrench and lay siege works around the fort, moving artillery to within five hundred yards or so of the fort's outer defensive wall. Rather than attempt a defense of the fort, under Gen. Montcalm's instructions, the French commander withdrew his forces, blowing the powder magazine and setting fires by way of sabotage as they left. Wooden structures were still burning and smoldering when Amherst and his army entered and occupied it the next day. They renamed the bastion Fort Ticonderoga. While the fort went on to play a prominent and more well-known role in the coming War of Independence, there was never again fought a major pitched battle at the site.

QUEBEC: THE BATTLE THAT CEDED NORTH AMERICA

After Gen. Amherst laid siege to and captured the French fortress of Louisburg on Cape Breton Island, he was named second-in-command to Lord Loudoun of British forces in North America. In the capture of Louisburg, young brigadier James Wolfe won accolades for his role in the battle. As a result, Wolfe was named commanding officer for the British assault on New France's fortress capital of Quebec. With a supporting naval force, Gen. Wolfe landed on the Isle of Orleans in June and by mid-July occupied the heights of Point Levis directly across the St. Lawrence from the city with a force of forty-five hundred experienced, disciplined redcoat regulars and several experienced, attached companies of Rogers' Rangers from New Hampshire.

On the northern shore of the river at Beauport, about eight miles downriver from the city, stood the French army encampment commanded by the Marquis de Montcalm. Very close in size to the British force, Gen. Montcalm's troops, however, included a high percentage of inexperienced Canadian militia and a smattering of their Indian allies.

For the next two months, the British directed a cannon bombardment against the city to weaken its defenses. Quebec was shattered with an estimated forty thousand shells and cannonballs. Women, children and old men were driven to the woods, and the city largely reduced to a mass of rubble.

By early September British ships had gained control of the St. Lawrence both upriver and downriver of Quebec. Wolfe determined that the time had come to strike. On the night of September 13th, he directed a highly risky amphibious landing, crossing the broad, swift river under cover of darkness to the base of 170-foot cliffs that the French had adjudged to be an impregnable natural defense. Such did not prove to be the case.

The Battle of Quebec, sometimes called the Battle of the Plains of Abraham, was over in half an hour.

Through the dark and dawn, Wolfe's infantry scaled the treacherous heights. By 8 a.m. his entire force was assembled in horseshoe formation across the Plains of Abraham. Hearing the news, Montcalm carelessly determined to attack before the British could occupy the lower city. Marshalling his troops in three tight ranks across the field from the British, in the set-piece fashion of eighteenth-century European warfare, Montcalm ordered the advance. His inexperienced troops began firing at the outer range of their low-caliber muskets. Wolfe's disciplined redcoats stood fast until the French were little more than forty yards from their lines. When the order came to fire, it only took a couple of volleys to crush and scatter the advancing French, who retreated through the city below.

The Battle of Quebec, sometimes called the Battle of the Plains of Abraham, was over in half an hour. Both Gen. Wolfe and the Marquis de Montcalm were mortally wounded in the affray. When Wolfe heard of his swift victory as he lay on the field, the young general is reported to have said, "God be praised, I will die in peace." The city formally surrendered on September 18th.

Five Great Fort Visits
Where the French and Indian War
Becomes Real

Fort Necessity, near Uniontown, Pennsylvania

Now a National Battlefield, the wooden stockade and fort that saw the first military engagement (with a twenty-one-year-old George Washington at command) in what would become the Seven Years' War sits on Route 40 (the National Road) a dozen miles east of Uniontown—about a two-hour drive from Pittsburgh.
www.nps.gov.us/fone

The Fort at No. 4, Charlestown, New Hampshire

On the banks of the Connecticut River, the fortified village of No. 4 was the northern and westernmost settlement in New England when settlers stockaded it in 1745. Subject to repeated Indian attacks, the fort became a staging ground for militia moving toward the Champlain Valley to fight the French and their Indian allies.
www.fortat4.org

Fort Ticonderoga, Ticonderoga, New York

Built to be an imposing and intimidating fortress, the French constructed Fort Carillon on a promontory over the narrows of Lake Champlain. Renamed Ticonderoga after the British and colonials took over, the massive complex with a significant garrison and artillery fire power proved an important strategic target in two wars.
www.fortticonderoga.org

Fort Beausejour, Aulac, New Brunswick

At the very head of the Bay of Fundy, Fort Beausejour holds commanding views over the narrow isthmus between Nova Scotia and New Brunswick. Its capture by the British in 1755 (who renamed it Fort Cumberland) severed a vital communications and supply line between Louisbourg and Quebec City.
www.pc.gc.ca

Beyond the earthwork ramparts of Fort Beausejour, the mist and fog hang low over the Bay of Fundy.

Fortress at Louisbourg, Cape Breton, Nova Scotia

What began as a growing French fishing and trading port was swallowed by enclosing fortifications that were the largest in North America and took twenty years to build (1720–1740). It was nonetheless taken twice—by the colonials in 1748 and again by British and colonial militia forces in 1758. Roughly a quarter of the original fortress has been reconstructed—still an impressive visit.
www.fortressoflouisbourg.ca

The Plains of Abraham spread across a 240-acre plateau on high ground just upriver on the St. Lawrence, overlooking the walls and streets of the eighteenth-century city and still amazingly "old world" today.

While the Battle of Quebec is regarded as decisive in finishing the war in North America, it was not quite the end. The surviving French army withdrew to Montreal to regroup through the winter. It returned in the spring with a force of five thousand under the command of Chevalier de Levis and defeated the smaller British army of Gen. James Murray in the Battle of Sainte Foy near a village some five miles west of Quebec. Levis could not consolidate his victory, however, as British ships overwhelmingly controlled the St. Lawrence, preventing any resupply of the French army, which was forced to withdraw back to Montreal. It was the last French victory in North America.

Skirmishes and acts of war may have continued through 1760, but the French were finished in New France. In September 1760 French governor Vaudreuil surrendered the province to Gen. Amherst in Montreal. In the negotiations, French colonists were given the right to retain their property and homes and to worship freely as Roman Catholics.

The Treaty of Paris in 1763 brought a formal end to the Seven Years' War. The French ceded all of New France to Britain with the exception of the two small islands of Miquelon and St. Pierre off the coast of Newfoundland (still French territories, with a combined population of six thousand). They also maintained their island possessions in the Caribbean—Guadeloupe and Martinique. Spain ceded Florida to Britain in exchange for the return of Cuba. The Spanish also received Louisiana from the French, and agreement was made that the Mississippi River be open for commerce to all nations.

Je Me Souviens

Throughout the Northeast, cars from the province of Quebec are a familiar sight with their white license plates adorned by the French fleur-de-lis and the legend *Je me souviens*.

In 1883 the architect Eugène-Étienne Taché had the phrase carved under the Quebec coat of arms above the main entrance to the provincial Parliament building in Quebec City: *Je me souviens*—"I Remember." It was soon adopted as the provincial motto. Though no official explanation was ever offered and the meaning of the expression has been controversially debated, Tache later expressed that his intention was to commemorate the panoply of heroes and memories of Quebec's history. The building's façade hosts statues honoring twenty-two people who were major figures in the province's history, including both Wolfe and Montcalm.

CHAPTER 19

Inching toward Independence

The four cornerstones of character on which the structure of this nation was built are: Initiative, Imagination, Individuality and Independence"

—EDDIE RICKENBACKER

PUSHING THE BOUNDARIES

As we have seen, by the early 1700s, the strategy for the growth of Virginia begun by Governor Berkeley back in the 1640s had built a prosperous colony. Plantations and farms radiated from the Tidewater inland across the Piedmont and now into the Shenandoah Valley. In 1699 the provincial capital had moved to higher ground at Williamsburg, named after the monarch, William III. Already the site of the colony's institution of higher education, the College of William & Mary, a capitol building was raised and an ambitious new town laid out. In Boston, Portsmouth, and Providence the governor had a "residence," in royalist Williamsburg, they built a Governor's Palace.

By the nature of Virginia's social structure, the wealth and political power in the colony, concentrated in the hands of its planter elite, gravitated to the attractive new capital. Williamsburg quickly became the social as well as the political center of Virginia. In 1728 the ambitious town formally received a charter as a city—the oldest such in English America.

We think of the thirteen American colonies in their present form. It's easy to forget that even in the mid-1700s—more than a century after serious colonization began—the majority of the population still remained very close to the coast. We have observed before that such inland settlements and communities that existed did so largely along the navigable rivers and their valleys.

The end of New France and elimination of the French presence to the north of the British colonies was celebrated in Britain as well as the colonies, ending what had been an ongoing defensive threat and expense. In London, much of the political credit accrued to William Pitt.

The years of war and disease took a severe toll on the native Indian tribes, as well, largely ending the Indian wars in the north. The colonial northwestern frontier pushed west. The 1760s saw a rapid expansion of communities west of the Connecticut River into Vermont, New York's Mohawk Valley, and northeast into Maine.

The British quickly realized that they could not hold what are now New Brunswick, Cape Breton, and mainland Nova Scotia as British

Aftermath: The Naming of Towns

With the end of the Seven Years' War and the opening up of land west of the Connecticut River for settlement, New Hampshire villages, towns, and farms spread west as well between the Merrimack Valley (a line today from Concord, Manchester, and Nashua) and the Connecticut River.

To the east of the Merrimack River and along the seacoast, almost all towns bear the name of English places—often the English towns that the original settlers left behind: Dover, Durham, Exeter, Portsmouth, Kensington, Epping, Rochester, Newmarket, Kingston, Newcastle, and such similar.

West of the Merrimack River, many of the townships are named for historic individuals of colonial years, early New Hampshire leaders, and Founding Fathers: Amherst, Walpole, Charlestown, Stark, Mason, Washington, Franklin, Weare, Bartlett, Webster, and others. Colonial governor Benning Wentworth was triple honored in the towns of Wentworth, Bennington, and neighboring Francestown, named after his wife.

territory without occupying the land. Small resident garrisons at Fort Louisbourg and Halifax would not do the job. A scheme was put forth to encourage English settlement of the province: Farmers were enticed with free land—and they went.

Between 1759 and 1768, some two thousand families from New England accepted the invitation and the land, uprooted, and relocated north to Nova Scotia and New Brunswick. Farmers settled along the Bay of Fundy coast; fishermen congregated on Nova Scotia's south shore. They became known as the Planters, the "first families" of British Atlantic Canada.

Paying the Piper

Back in London, the end of the Seven Years' War resulted in other consequences, however. George III had succeeded his grandfather as king in October 1760 at the tender age of twenty-two. His first years were marked by political upheaval in the Commons over the resolution of the 1763 Treaty of Paris and its aftermath.

It was only just that the colonies bear some of the burden of this expense and the resultant national debt.

Foreign wars are expensive. It cost hugely to equip, supply, support, and transport on eighteenth-century ships armies in the North American theater. While trade with the colonies was certainly enriching the mother country's coffers to some extent, British politicians (whose own wealth was inevitably land-based) found little direct benefit to Britain from absorbing the expense of the war. The Seven Years' War, in both North America and Europe, had doubled Britain's national debt.

It seemed quite reasonable to the Whig prime minister George Grenville and other leaders of Parliament as well as the ministers and advisors of King George III that the colonials themselves bear part of the costs of their own security. After all, Britain had just sent armies of soldiers and flotillas of ships to their North American colonies at great expense to defend the colonists and their property. In fact, for a century, British ships had guaranteed trade, commerce, and lifelines to the mother country. It was only just that the colonies bear some of the burden of this expense and the resultant national debt. From this difference in perspective great events soon transpired.

PRELUDES TO THE WAR OF INDEPENDENCE

The popular narrative of American history really picks up here, in the run-up to the Revolutionary War in the 1770s. It has been well studied and well written about by both academic and popular historians, and by poets and screenwriters.

A series of new taxes imposed on the colonies was put forth to help pay off the war's debt, most famously in the 1765 Stamp Acts. The familiar rallying cry was "No taxation without representation!" That certainly sounds axiomatic to us today; it just sounds fair to our democratic ears. A British Parliament and the ministers surrounding King George III saw it differently. It would be an understatement to say that the imposition of these taxes was not popular, and was defied, in the colonies.

By 1770 the population of the British colonies was more than two million, with Virginia alone accounting for almost 450,000. Pennsylvania and Massachusetts each had nearly 250,000. The smallest colony in population was also the youngest; Georgia numbered about 23,000 colonials. In seven decades, however, the colonies' population had multiplied by a factor of ten.

Many old established families had been in the colonies now for several generations. Their primary loyalties had become local and to their colony rather than to a Britain across the sea that they had never known. The steady stream of new arrivals to North American shores brought with them a constant influx of new ideas, and the intellectual crosscurrents sweeping through Europe in the eighteenth century.

In various forms across Western Europe, what intellectual history knows as the "Age of Reason," or, more broadly, "The Enlightenment" was well underway. Generations had passed since the Reformation effectively broke the intellectual hegemony of the medieval Catholic Church. By the end of the seventeenth century, the religious wars were largely over, and the medieval worldview that had been broadly shared across Europe just failed to explain the reality of the world, for Protestant and Catholic alike. Every area of philosophy and human life suddenly appeared open for examination anew.

In broadest terms, society began rethinking itself: science and an interest in the natural world, government, and the structure of society; the nature of reason and the mechanism of knowledge; ethics and the very existence of God. All came into question, and brilliant thinkers seizing the challenge redefined the world we take for granted. Nowhere in Europe did this flame of Enlightenment burn brighter than in Britain.

In the century between Thomas Hobbes's publication of *Leviathan* in 1651 and Adam Smith's *The Wealth of Nations* in 1776, Sir Isaac Newton and David Hume laid the foundation for empirical science. John Locke's *Two Treatises of Government* (1689) challenged the relationship between the state and the individual, emphasizing personal liberty and the rights of property.

Down in the East Sussex, England, market town of Lewes, Thomas Paine earned a reputation as a debater and political thinker. A plaque at the entrance of the White Hart Hotel in Lewes proclaims: "Thomas Paine here expounded his revolutionary politics (1737–1809). This inn is regarded a cradle of American independence which he helped to found with pen and sword." Even Benjamin Franklin was impressed, took him under his wing, and championed Paine's *Common Sense* and *The Age of Reason*.

Every shipload of new arrivals to Charleston, Philadelphia, or Providence brought new ideas to be debated in coffeehouses and taverns through the colonies. Among the most influential writers bruited about in the colonies, as well, was the French thinker Montesquieu, who argued for a separation of powers in government. Together, these natural and political philosophers and many others created the currents of thought and conversation in a nascent world that had no old order to sweep away. Thomas Jefferson and Benjamin Franklin, Samuel Adams and James Madison, again among many others, found the inspiration and ideas that filled our founding documents and defined the uniqueness of our emerging nation.

Colonial Williamsburg Takes the Stage

This is where colonial Williamsburg enters the narrative. Settled as an outpost of Jamestown in 1638, and then called Middle Plantation, the seat of the College of William & Mary was a natural place to move the colonial government when Jamestown's statehouse burned down in 1698. The new capital was duly renamed Williamsburg to honor King William III. In the 1770s Williamsburg was the height of colonial fashion and Virginia social life. It was also the seat of government of the largest, most populous of the thirteen provinces. And revolution was in the air.

This is the period of colonial history depicted today at Colonial Williamsburg, the most complete and extensive living history museum of our colonial history. The re-creation and restoration of the early Virginia capital was the brainchild of the rector at historic Bruton Parish Church, Rev. W. A. R. Goodwin, who convinced philanthropist John D. Rockefeller to take an interest in and largely fund the massive project, beginning in the late 1920s. Over the years, the foundation Rockefeller established has restored or re-created hundreds of structures, more than eighty of them original colonial-era buildings. From the Governor's Palace to the capitol, from Chowning's Tavern and all along Duke of Gloucester Street, reenactors create life in the Georgian provincial capital, and revolution is in the air.

In the middle of the peninsula created by the James and York Rivers, Williamsburg is some eight miles from historic Jamestown and a dozen from Yorktown, scene of the British surrender to Washington and the colonial army in 1783. The three epic scenes of American colonial history are connected by the scenic Colonial National Historic Parkway.

The colorful run-up to the revolution is well-known, filled with events such as the Boston Tea Party, the Boston Massacre, the calling of the Continental Congress in 1775, the ride of Paul Revere, and such.

Just a few years before, though, the American colonies were enthusiastic champions of the Hanoverian monarchy, thoroughly integrated into the British Empire in every way except their oceanic separation. In New

York and on Williamsburg's Duke of Gloucester Street, ladies paraded in the up-to-date fashions just off the boat from London. The ship also brought London newspapers, books, fabrics, and china. Philadelphia was the second largest city in the empire, and Boston and New York among Britain's most important trading ports. Our principal colonial towns and cities were growing, wealthy places of trade, civil organization, and a community life the equal of such places across the mother country.

Our American popular imagination conceives of our eighteenth-century identity in vaguely log-cabin terms. We were the rustic pioneer farmers, who rallied to beat off the snobbish, bullying English masters and have our freedom. That's not really an accurate generalization. Ironically, however, that's just the way the English power classes of the time tended to view us as well.

The transfer of social capital between England and the American colonies didn't flow both ways. We were still the colonies; though the

While our principal port towns along the seacoast emulated Georgian life, fashions, and architecture in England, those settling our expanding frontier south and west did live in log cabins, like this 1734 log cabin on the grounds of Abram's Delight in upper Shenandoah Valley.

influence of English society came naturally to us, it did not flow back. Most of the Georgian aristocracy and gentry would have possessed little detailed knowledge of American life (and little curiosity to know). Vague stereotypes about the rustic colonials were easy to imagine, and just as easy to create.

At the same time, it is not difficult to see why the English upper classes would have seen us as somewhat easily dismissed relations. A colonial capital such as Philadelphia boasted street after street of expansive Georgian townhouses in the latest Palladian and Federalist architectural styles. From Portsmouth to Savannah, our port-of-entry towns from New Hampshire to Georgia enjoyed a prosperous "contemporary" life. In truth, there weren't very many of those, however, and they would hardly have looked particularly impressive to aristocratic visitors from abroad. Our colonial society was well developed, and our common citizenry was perhaps better informed than our European counterparts. In comparison to

While our frontier self-image certainly included the log cabin in the 1700s, back in England, the decision makers spent months of the year residing and socializing in Bath and its elegant Georgian terraces like the Royal Crescent. It is little wonder they thought of us as rather rustic.

Bath's elegant limestone crescents and public buildings, or the Georgian terraces of South Kensington and Edinburgh, though, we might look rather small potatoes indeed.

The 1770s provide the end of the story, or, rather, the beginning. Here is where the narrative of American history picks up, when we begin to remember what happened because it is taught in grade school and every high school in America. We have not forgotten Washington and Jefferson, Ben Franklin, John Adams, and Alexander Hamilton; their faces appear on our currency, and towns in nearly every early state bear their names. The confrontation at Lexington and Concord, the winter of Valley Forge, and the British surrender at Yorktown are part of our national memory. The events of those years are part of our popular culture—*The Patriot*, "Yankee Doodle Dandy," and *1776*.

The struggle to make common cause in an underdog war, the leaders and visionaries on the many fronts of the war, its termination and the long compromising efforts that resulted in the Constitution of the United States composed in the Philadelphia constitutional convention are where American history traditionally begins.

And so every Fourth of July, Americans of every national background, ethnicity, and cultural history commemorate the proclamation of the Declaration of Independence: Independence Day. We splash red, white, and blue, shoot off fireworks, parade, and barbecue chickens to celebrate our nation on America's birthday. Except that it didn't quite happen that way.

France Supports Our Struggle?

Yes, the Marquis de Lafayette was a true believer in the nobility of the American cause for independence. France's aid to the American Revolutionary War effort was motivated far more, however, by the truth of the old adage: "The enemy of my enemy is my friend." The wars between Britain and France were not yet over, and the independence of the American colonies would, after all, weaken France's perennial enemy.

The Congressional Congress that gathered in Philadelphia the summer of 1776 was constituted of delegates from thirteen individual, self-governing colonies. Each of them arrived with specific instructions from their own colonial assemblies, and acted on its behalf. When the assembled delegates presented a united proclamation on July 4th they were speaking as a collective voice for thirteen individual, and by now surprisingly diverse, colonies.

A good old-fashioned patriotic holiday is Independence Day and long may she wave. But it's not really America's birthday; it's the anniversary of when the colonies formally declared their united intention to be independent of Great Britain. What followed, of course, was the War of Independence. It ended formally when the Treaty of Paris, signed in September 1783, was concluded between Great Britain and the colonial Congress.

None of the individuals present in Philadelphia that July that were signatories to the Declaration of Independence, from John Hancock and Thomas Jefferson, to Caesar Rodney and Josiah Bartlett, could have predicted the outcome of the next seven years of conflict needed to make that Declaration a reality. Let alone could they have foreseen the coming together of their colonies as a federal union in the fashion defined by the Constitution a decade later in 1786.

The United States of America began, however, when the Constitution coming out of the Philadelphia convention called to establish it was sent back to the colonies to ratify. The provision agreed was that the Constitution would be adopted, the colonies would become states and the federal United States born with the ratification of two-thirds of the colonies—nine. Month by month through the spring of 1786 colonial assemblies met, debated, and voted to ratify the Constitution. As their state license plate reminds us, the first to ratify was Delaware. On June 22, 1786, New Hampshire became the ninth colony to so vote, and the United States of America was born.

That's rather fitting. New Hampshire had been the first colony to declare independence and the first to adopt its own state constitution.

Where the Piscataqua River estuary opens into the Atlantic, the British fortified a rocky promontory in 1632 to protect access to Portsmouth harbor. Renamed Fort William and Mary, the manned British fort served as New Hampshire's colonial militia munitions depot as well. In December 1774 local Sons of Liberty raided the fort, seized the powder, small arms, and cannon and distributed them in several area towns—including a powder house in Exeter still standing on the banks of the Squamscot River. It was the first military action of the colonial rebellion.

The next June, powder and cannon were taken south to Boston, and put to use at the Battle of Bunker Hill.

Seven Founding Colonial Fathers

Everyone has heard of the Founding Fathers as a group, and a good percentage of Americans can recall at least a couple of names—Benjamin Franklin, George Washington, and so forth. They were certainly the founding leaders of what became our American federal republic. But our collective history preceded them by two centuries at least, built by many founders. Here are seven important colonial fathers that ought not to be forgotten.

Bartholomew Gosnold—No one was more personally vested in American colonization

William Brewster—From Scrooby Manor to Plymouth, the Elder of the Pilgrim community

John Cotton—Godfather of Massachusetts Bay Colony and architect of the New England Way

Roger Williams—The colonies' first Nonconformist became an exile to Rhode Island

Sir William Berkeley—Had the vision, persistence, and political skill to build Virginia

William Penn—Built tolerance, wisdom, and conscience into Quaker Pennsylvania

James Oglethorpe—Though his ideals did not last, had the insight and ability to plant Georgia as the first Enlightenment colony

Chapter 20

We Are the Epilogue

We have it in our power to build the world anew.

—Thomas Paine

Well, that's the backstory of America. Our "prehistory" is a part of our history. Our epilogue is the nation that resulted.

Ultimately, the independence of the American colonies from Great Britain was inevitable. It was only a matter of time and circumstance. Britain's heavy-handed use of the colonies in the aftermath of the Seven Years' War and the increasing spread of the then revolutionary new notions of government and the rights of individuals and their equality before law created both. All of the other principal settler colonies of what we know as the British Empire found their independence peacefully from the mother country via one route or another—Canada, Australia, New Zealand. Not all of Britain's imperial possessions found their way so peacefully.

To the extent that there are conclusions to be drawn, one strong current that emerges is how much the regional cultural distinctions between our North and South found their roots in the differences between the religious convictions and worldviews of their seventeeth-century settlement. These regional characteristics in social order and popular culture have inevitably lessened in the last two generations with the increasing homogenization of society as a result of information-age technology from television to smartphone. Nonetheless, these differences are certainly still pronounced, particularly outside metropolitan areas. Travel seventy miles from Atlanta or Boston and it's a different world.

T. S. Eliot's observation that the regional culture anywhere is largely defined by the dominant religious institution rings true. Even if the faith and belief system ceases to be the spiritual conviction of the majority, its residual impact upon society and social behaviors remains. Within the states that comprised colonial America, the differences in local culture between the North, the mid-Atlantic, and the South—again, certainly outside of the principal cities—illustrate that today.

In his political history *Liberty and Freedom*, David Hackett Fischer points out sagaciously that the southern colonies and the northern colonies were not fighting for the same thing in our American War of Independence. With its roots in the royalist, Anglican cause, the voices speaking for Virginia and her southern neighbors cried for "Liberty." They sought the traditional liberties of the English aristocracy and land-owning class. The firebrands of the northern colonies, however, were fighting for the "Freedom" of individual citizens.

Jude Hale would have been a teenager of sixteen when he fought at Bunker Hill. After seven years of soldiering with the Continental Army, he came home to Exeter at twenty-three.

Back in the Winter St. Cemetery in Exeter, lying a hundred yards from Maj. Gen. Nathaniel Folsom, is one of the lesser ranked soldiers. Jude Hale's story is etched on his memorial. Hale was an enslaved person in neighboring Kensington. At age sixteen, he fought in the Battle of Bunker Hill, and continued as a Continental soldier through the rest of the war until 1783. Hale returned to Exeter after the war a free man, married; he built a farm on Drinkwater Road, and died in 1814. Jude Hale fought for freedom. You're just not apt to find a tombstone like that in the South.

The regions were separated by New Jersey, Maryland, and the Quaker colony of Pennsylvania, and the mentality and temperament of William Penn's religious and political ideals—including tolerance and moderation. This was certainly a "third way" that provided a buffer zone between North and South. It may be one of the great providential acts of history that the Continental Congress and Constitutional Convention were held in Philadelphia, conducive to the compromises necessary in both fateful deliberations.

While the parallels are limited, historians have observed that at one level the War Between the States only a few generations later was a replay of the English Civil War that had spurred settlement and defined regional character here two hundred years earlier. Though the proximate causes were different, the opposing sides were fundamentally fighting the same war as their ancestors; their armies motivated and led the same way.

With an eye back on our colonial history, however, I am persuaded that there is certainly some truth in Jefferson Davis's observation: "It is not differences of opinion; it is the geographical lines, rivers and mountains which divide State from State, and make different nations of mankind."

THE FORGOTTEN FOUNDING FATHERS

We generally think of the "Founding Fathers" as those legendary figures who gave us the Declaration of Independence, fought the war that resulted, and gave us the U.S. Constitution—George Washington, Benjamin Franklin, Sam Adams, Thomas Jefferson, and so forth. Another thread in the narrative of our founding, however, seems to reveal several other individuals who deserve a bigger spotlight in American history.

In a sense, it all began with Bartholomew Gosnold, who has proved underrated by history as a visionary for England's colonial settlement. He charted Atlantic Canada and New England, organized the attempted colonization of Elizabeth Island in 1602, and subsequently played a lead in the Virginia Corporation and the foundation of Jamestown. Too bad he died young. One of the few places Gosnold is remembered is in the naming of the Gosnold Inn near Pemaquid Point, Maine. And in the garden close of St. Edmundsbury Cathedral in Bury St. Edmund, Suffolk,

The abstract sculpture in the St. Edmundsbury Cathedral close represents the *Godspeed*, which Goswold captained on the settlement voyage to Jamestown.

a place with which Gosnold was very familiar, stands a contemporary sculpture to his memory.

John Cotton, though he appears to be a quiet figure in the history, largely inspired the 1630 foundation of Massachusetts Bay Colony from the pulpit of St. Botolph's Church, Boston, Lincolnshire. He followed the exodus to Massachusetts as a respected leader and authored the book that became the defining handbook of New England Congregationalism—what was also known as the New England Way.

When Sir William Berkeley was appointed governor of Virginia in 1641, the colony was still something of a struggling backwater, its survival as a colony not even assured. Berkeley's leadership, personal political skills, and vision over thirty-five years built Virginia into the richest, most populous English possession in North America. That's an incredible accomplishment by any measure.

There were also key active players who influenced the character and destiny of what became the thirteen colonies that united to stand for independence in the 1770s—some of whom never set foot in the colonies, or never identified with them: Roger Williams, Lord George Calvert, Gen. Jeffrey Amherst and Gen. James Wolfe, John Mason, William Penn, and James Oglethorpe come to mind.

No, none of these men were present, active contributors at the eighteenth-century birth of our nation. But they were all certainly significant figures in the founding of this country and what has become of it.

GO WEST, YOUNG COUNTRY

After nationhood for America, our continuing narrative was Manifest Destiny. State by state the nation grew west across the continent to the Pacific—America the beautiful, from sea to shining sea. Throughout the nineteenth century, the "huddled masses" came from the nations of Europe and Asia as economic migrants, political and religious refugees, just as did our colonial predecessors. They brought colloquialisms and cuisines, music and myths that would enrich the ever more colorful fabric of American society—a society that would have been totally incomprehensible to those seventeenth-century English settlers.

It is right and proper to celebrate our cultural diversity, reflecting the broad spectrum of human experience that America has welcomed with open arms. Alas, in the process, we seem to have largely ignored, if not denigrated, the heritage of the British Renaissance and Reformation that is our united legacy.

The English language, embraced by a dozen generations of immigrant peoples, gives us the vernacular Bible, Shakespeare, Jane Austen, and Charles Dickens that became the fount of Herman Melville, Mark Twain, Emily Dickinson, and Robert Frost. If we are Episcopalian, Congregationalist, Methodist, Presbyterian, or Quaker, our spiritual roots are anchored in Britain. Institutions we take for granted—Boy Scouts, the YMCA, and the Salvation Army, for instance—have their founding in England. We march down our graduation aisles to the music of Edward Elgar, and our wedding aisles to Henry Purcell, and stand (as did King George II) for Handel's "Hallelujah Chorus." And it is estimated that some thirty million Americans can trace their ancestry to the *Mayflower*.

The cultural cross-pollination now works two ways, with Broadway and London's West End sharing the stage, and with music, movie, and media personalities popular on both sides of the Atlantic. Americans have long had an ongoing fascination with the Royal Family and the Beatles, while Brits happily munch McDonald's burgers and KFC.

A WELCOME IN THE VALLEYS

The Welsh claim that there is no real translation for the Welsh word *hiraeth*. It describes a feeling of longing that is akin to homesickness. A nostalgia for what is known in the blood or a deep subconscious yearning for tribe or homeland. Every Welsh male voice choir includes in its repertoire "There'll be a Welcome in the Valleys."

> "This land of song will keep a welcome.
> And with a love that never fails,
> We'll kiss away each hour of hiraeth
> When you come home again to Wales."

However *hiraeth* might best be explained, the Celtic peoples all seem to share the characteristic in substantive amounts—the Welsh no more than the Irish and Scots. Expatriate Scots and Irish across "the colonies"—no matter how many generations ago their kin immigrated to these shores—still feel a kinship identity to their ancestral homeland. It shows up on St. Patrick's Day and in the popularity of Irish pubs, Scots clan societies, St. Andrews organizations, and Highland Games across the country.

The English, who dominated the British Isles in arms, population, wealth, and world influence for ten centuries, played a similarly prominent role (understandably enough) in our colonial history and cultural formation. Whether recent expats from Bournemouth or Birmingham or descendents of the families who first settled Massachusetts Bay, however, those of Anglo-Saxon, Viking, Norman ilk that we know as "English" generally seem deficient in the *hiraeth* gene.

That often changes remarkably for folks when they make the Atlantic crossing, a little more comfortably than our ancestors did. Many

Americans traveling to Britain for the first time, especially those who venture far from cosmopolitan London, report feeling a strange homecoming in Britain. Though it is not home, there is a sense of familiarity and belonging. Even Americans whose own ancestry came from Korea, Calcutta, or Constantinople appreciate that glint of recognition that this is familiar homeland.

Year after year, we go back. More Americans travel to Great Britain than to any other transoceanic destination. We visit stately homes and palaces, castles and cathedrals, battlefields, gardens and pubs, and the homes of writers, musicians, and statesmen in the land and landscapes that inspired them. In sum, we travel to Britain for the history, and because we recognize at some deep, quiet level that it is part of our own history.

Though our democracies developed differently, with their own growing pains, the spiritual and political roots of the United Kingdom and the United States are shared. The often-spoken-of "special relationship" between our nations finds its wellspring here.

APPENDIX

A Time Line of Colonial Events

1497—John Cabot discovers the coast of North America

1587—Sir Walter Raleigh attempts and fails at the lost colony of Roanoke Island

1607—The successful (barely) plantation of a first permanent English settlement on Jamestown Island

1608—Samuel Champlain establishes the colony of New France at Quebec City

1620—The self-exiled Pilgrims and company land the *Mayflower* at Plymouth

1630—Massachusetts Bay Colony begins with a Puritan flotilla

1642—Parliament and the king come to arms in the English Civil War

1650—The Puritan Commonwealth changes colonial migration

1660—Restoration of the monarchy turns the New World wheel

1675—King Philip's bloody War

1682—William Penn's first colonists arrive in Pennsylvania

1716—Settlement begins in the Backcountry

1733—The establishment of Georgia completes the thirteen colonies

1744—King George's War: only a prelude

1754—French and Indians: the Seven Years' War begins

1759—Battle of Quebec decides the end of New France

1765—The Stamp Act begins America's march to independence

INDEX

Abenaki Indians, 133–35, *135*, 172
Acadians, 176
Adams, John, 202
Adams, Samuel, 198
Age of Reason, 197
The Age of Reason (Paine), 198
Algonquin Indians, 53
American prehistory, viii, 1–2, 209–11
Americans: independence history of, 202; roots of, vii–viii, 209–11; Scots-Irish shaping, 168–69
American War of Independence: Folsom in, 174, *174*; North and South differences on, 205–7, *206*
Anabaptists, 71, 123, 154, 162
Anglican Church, 126, 144. *See also* Church of England
Anglo-Catholic Church, 40, 113
Anglo-Indian treaty, 93
Anne, 154
Antinomian or Free Grace Controversy, 72–73, 75
Appalachian mountains, 162–68
Atlantic colonies, 27–28, 90; Congregationalists and Presbyterians in, 105; East Midlands battle and, 8, 10–11

Backcountry: Lederer exploring, 153–54; Scots, Scots-Irish and fourth Great Migration to, 154, 161–62; for Scots-Irish colonists, 154, 161–62, 164–67, 169, 212; Shenandoah Valley as, 212; Washington, G., surveying, 178
Bacon, Nathaniel, 116
Baltimore, Maryland, 82
Baptist Church, 71, 144, 146
Bath, England, *201*
Battle of Culloden, 158
Battle of Quebec, 212. *See also* Quebec City
Berkeley, William: Bacon's Rebellion and, 116; on education and disobedience, 142; as founding father, 204, 208; Virginia royal refuge by, 91–93, 101–2, 126; west Virginia expeditions by, 153
Bible, 18–19, 33–36, 73
Boston, England, 62, *63*, 64, 66, *66*, 67
Boston, Massachusetts: Cotton emigrating to, 69; largest town in, 130–31; outer Massachusetts remove from, 87
Braddock, Edward, 176